The Association for F
is delighted
The Change /

APM
Association for
Project Management

Project professionals and the projects they are delivering play an essential role in tackling the many complex issues facing our world today. From food security and post-conflict capacity building to health equality and environmental sustainability, projects are central to delivering the solutions we need.

The significant achievements of project professionals are, unfortunately, often overshadowed by media reports of project failure. This is why opportunities to celebrate project success, such as the Change Awards 2024, are so important. It is right that we shine a light on the change-makers focused on improving the world we live in.

We should all support our project profession to deliver the change that is needed. Why? Because when projects succeed, society benefits.

Professor Adam Boddison OBE, APM Chief Executive

This book is a must read for people who actually want to lead organizations to a better place for clients, their teams and the wellbeing of the organizations they run... I loved this book and will share it with all my colleagues because it is emotionally intelligent and has humour going through it like Brighton through rock. More than that, it presents really interesting ways of discussing what innovation is... [Tammy's] art is the art of refining the question that needs to be asked to define the problem that needs solving.

Sir Tim Smit – Lost Gardens of Heligan and the Eden Project

Dr Tammy Watchorn combines the latest thinking in change management to respond to the evolving environment in which we deliver change, and she does it in a way that harks back to the adventure books from childhood that allow you to choose your path and learn from your decisions. If all learning was this enjoyable, we would all spend much more time invested in it.

Jo Stanford – Head of Project Profession, NHS

I really like the engaging and immersive nature of the book told in a novel style. I felt like I was on the journey every step of the way... and the quiz was a great way to summarize a kind of 'playbook'. I will return to use it.

Rob Cole – project and programme change specialist, Three UK

Thank you for writing this book! *The Change Ninja Handbook* is relatable on so many levels, an easy and entertaining read. It brings to life characters we all know from experience and takes a helpful and practical approach to effecting change. I was inspired by the writer's courage to do things differently and to share their experiences to help others. It certainly helped me.

Shara Seeyave – Executive Director of Human Resources, MSCI

The Change Ninja. What can I say… amazing. Not only did I learn how to manage change more effectively, I also laughed out loud… this book is so funny and informative.

Annmarie Sanderson – Programme Manager, NHS

Finally, a chance to try out those tricky decisions before you have to make them at work in real life! An absolute joy to read whilst picking up actual, tangible tools to lead change.

Molly Thomas – NHS Health Education England

When I was a kid I loved books like this: if you made the right choices you could thwart the wicked wizard or slay the awful dragon. Now with this cunning, entertaining and brilliant book, you can slay the toughest dragon of our working life, the dragon called change. Loved it.

Geoff Burch – business guru, bestselling author, TV presenter and award-winning communicator

The Change Ninja Handbook provides a set of engaging and accessible insights into the world of change leadership. Tammy skilfully gives the reader permission to navigate their own course through the various change challenges that are posed. This handbook is an essential guide for any professional interested in understanding how to implement and influence change. From stakeholder engagement and creativity to digital transformation and innovation, *The Change Ninja Handbook* will help to lead you to a solution.

Prof Adam Boddison – Chief Executive, Association for Project Management

A fantastically entertaining and amusing book on change management that almost never mentions management. Instead, using a 'choose your own adventure' style, this book is an inspired way of learning about change as you get to take risks, try things out and improve your ninja skills of stealth and perseverance.

Paul Taylor – Innovation Service Design, Bromford

Original format, refreshing and relatable style, would leave any potential Change Ninja rushing out to try a new and inspiring approach – love it!

Sarah Bunting – Senior Programme Manager, London Stock Exchange Group

I loved the two realities presented at every step of the change journey in this book. Being able to consider what a poor response and a good response to a wide variety of common change challenges looks like really brings the challenges of change management to life. I highly recommend this book as an excellent read.

Melanie Franklin – Agile Change Management and APMG International

I loved this book – fast, funny and real world. Most organizations lie: they don't actually want change, they only want the benefits of change. This book shows you how to survive being a 'change leader' in a world where governance, process and compliance seem to be against you. A practical, interactive and FUN book!

Stephen Carver – senior lecturer, consultant and speaker in change and crisis management at Cranfield University School of Management

This book is a riot. A provocative W1A adventure through the theatre of 'change management', except this time you get to be the protagonist. Tammy Watchorn knows the pitfalls of dull frameworks and theories and so gives readers agency and the opposite experience of being trapped in a landlocked meeting. Guaranteed, this book will help you to understand why things never actually seem to change, and what you can do differently.

Alex Barker – coach, facilitator, speaker and author of How to Be More Pirate

This book is a technology for change, with just the right wicked sense of humour it needs to get past the dour gatekeepers of change management. A much-needed, wry look at how to take work apart and make it better.

Sam Conniff – documentary maker, social enterprise starter, award winner and author of Be More Pirate *and* How to Be More Pirate

the Change Ninja HANDBOOK

An interactive adventure for leading change

Dr Tammy Watchorn

First published in Great Britain by Practical Inspiration Publishing, 2022

© Tammy Watchorn, 2022

The moral rights of the author have been asserted

ISBN   9781788603706 (print)
        9781788603720 (epub)
        9781788603713 (mobi)

All rights reserved. This book, or any portion thereof, may not be reproduced without the express written permission of the author.

Every effort has been made to trace copyright holders and to obtain their permission for the use of copyright material. The publisher apologizes for any errors or omissions and would be grateful if notified of any corrections that should be incorporated in future reprints or editions of this book.

Illustrations by Vanessa Randle

Want to bulk-buy copies of this book for your team and colleagues? We can introduce case studies, customize the content and co-brand *The Change Ninja Handbook* to suit your business's needs.

Please email info@practicalinspiration.com for more details.

Practical Inspiration Publishing

MIX
Paper | Supporting responsible forestry
FSC® C013604

For the Coopers and McGoo

Table of contents

Foreword by Eddie Obeng.. *xi*
Preface.. *xv*
Once upon a time 1
How to play 5
Characters.. 7
Challenge 1: Innovation workshop 15
Sami's Fables Part 1 28
Challenge 2: Creating space 38
Sami's Fables Part 2 47
Challenge 3: I didn't sign up for this 53
Sami's Fables Part 3 60
Challenge 4: Well, that does look innovative............67
Sami's Fables Part 4 80
Challenge 5: Virtually virtual......................................89
Sami's Fables Part 5 99
Challenge 6: Take two 109
Sami's Fables Part 6 123
Challenge 7: Shall we just do what we always
do and expect different results? 140
Sami's Fables Part 7 144

Challenge 7: Continued...154
Challenge 8: Too serious to play...........................160
Sami's Fables Part 8 174
Challenge 9: Beating the drum 184
Sami's Fables Part 9 192
Challenge 9: Continued...215
Sami's Fables Part 10 220
Challenge 10: Hack to the future............................231
Is it Game Over? 237
Appendix of tools 241
Recommended reading...243
Useful resources, methods and toolkits..................245
Acknowledgements 247

Foreword
by Eddie Obeng

You, like me, will know that 'when a story is told it cannot but grow old'. And we all know that with grown-ups retelling the story the same way makes it unsurprising and ineffective. For decades now we've listened to keynotes on change. We've participated in workshops on change management. We've read case stories about projects and programmes, dreaming of the successes others have seemed to so effortlessly achieve. We've bought shelf loads of self-help books, textbooks and bodies of knowledge compilations, each promising the same. And in the evenings, we've browsed blogs that provide personal perspectives. And yet our projects remain not perfect. Our programmes have hidden problems. And our agenda for change is still stock full of challenges.

Tammy Watchorn has managed to do two things to refresh the story, to inspire you and enable you to act differently. It's a richer story. You will quickly realize that she has cunningly woven into the tale her personal experiences. She seems to have chosen ones that provide humour and lightness to the tough challenges faced in delivering change. That is a wonderful relief and tells the story anew in a way that, I believe, will grip your imagination.

You begin reading. You reach page 5, 'How to play'. You skim read it, not really absorbing the implications and meaning of what is written there. It takes you up to page 20 to suddenly come of age and realize that *you* are in control of the story line. You have to decide what you do and as a result what happens to you next on your Ninja journey. In a world of increasing tramlines, hoops to jump through, metrics and qualifications you suddenly have autonomy and agency. Life is once again an adventure. I loved that.

I did everything I could to try to persuade Tammy not to write a book. I explained all the pitfalls. How it would fall upon the top of the mountain of 'samey' books that everyone puts on their shelves but make no difference to the fabric of reality, as it slipped and slithered down the slopes rapidly covered up by even more 'samey' books! But she was determined. So imagine my joy and surprise when I realized she had created something unique and different – a truly customer-driven learning handbook. You will feel the same joy and surprise as you venture into the book. Will you make decisions that damage your health to the point where you lose life after life? Or will you play with a mindset that life is too short not to do it right and best as fast as you can, once? Either way you'll be able to track your progress.

I get to have a cameo/walk-on part as the 'Boffin-Prof'. She should have said, but didn't, so I will, 'Any resemblance that this character bears to persons living or dead is mere coincidence!'

This book bears little resemblance to stories of the past. Ninja-like, it reaches a higher level by climbing up the wall and entering through a window instead of using the lift or stairs like everyone else. Enjoy having your interest and passion for change renewed.

Eddie
Prof. Eddie Obeng
MyQubicle | Pentacle campus| QUBE | https://QUBE.cc
07 March 2020

Preface

Working as a change leader in a large public sector organization I often found myself asking 'is it me?' while scratching my head at the seemingly illogical decisions and processes that seemed purposefully designed to block you doing what you'd been asked to do. It was almost as if you were being tested to see how far you could actually get before the big 'Game Over' sign flashed up. I naively assumed it was just my organization, but when I started working more at a national level across different organizations, I quickly realized that it wasn't me and it wasn't just my organization.

It could often seem that people, individuals, were determined to prevent progress but I soon recognized that, other than one or two, most people were just trying to do the job they'd been asked to do to the best of their abilities. It was the system that had, over the years, based on what seemed like some ancient laws, turned into such a convoluted and complex spider's web that no one could really untangle anything. People were just following what they assumed to be the right process and (wrongly) assumed they made sense to someone somewhere.

This complex intertangled web meant leading change was more about navigating roadblock after roadblock while trying not to forget what the overall mission and goal was. Add to that the stream of new vision statements, latest buzzwords and leadership fads and I realized just how hard it could be to do anything and how easy it could be to just give up like many had done before.

But I discovered that, with some tenacity, lots of learning, a will to try, accepting you might get things wrong, try again and being able to see the humour in the illogic, it *was* possible to do some good things. However, making stealth-like moves, often under the radar, was, it often seemed to me, the only way to get things done. To become, in fact, a Change Ninja. I also discovered the necessity to seek out a like-minded crew en route to help keep resilience and spirits high when needed. And gin helped.

The stories in this adventure book are real. But as with any story they're only told from one perspective. Anyone who was there at the time may recall them in different ways.

The people I mention, however, aren't real. They're fictional characters. It would be cruel and possibly slanderous if they were based on real people.

Also, the stories aren't about pointing fingers at who said what or who did what. It's about trying to understand how to navigate the challenges that the system routinely throws at us and how to use different approaches, tools and ways of working to help us lead change and deliver outcomes despite these challenges.

These stories are interactive, allowing you to make choices on what you'd do in these scenarios. You may get it right first time. You may fail quickly. But you, like me, will learn as you go. These are my stories, but they're not unique. They happen in every organization. Over and over again.

One final note. These stories all happened pre-Covid. Since then, the digital workforce has become very much a forced way of working for many and never has there been a more urgent burning platform for finding new ways of working. Sadly, the reality for many is that. While things such as Zoom and MS Teams have allowed remote and digital working, the actual way of working is still pretty much the same. The need for meetings, papers and email was just lifted and exacerbated in the Zoom world.

The commute time, which everyone previously complained about, was suddenly filled with more meetings to the point where everyone is now clamouring to commute again just for some peace. For many the opportunity to really change how everyone worked wasn't fully grasped and I suspect that the changes we need in how we work are now even harder to put in place than before. And this means we need Ninjas. Change Ninjas. And lots of them.

Once upon a time

Once upon a time in a land far away, there was drive for organizational change. To be more agile, to be more digital, to become innovative, to empower staff and, most importantly, *to transform*. It was a big challenge and one that required bravery, resilience, new ideas, creativity and, more importantly, a real will to actually change.

It sounds exciting, doesn't it?

And the best bit?

You work in this organization.

And you're getting a bit fidgety and looking for a new challenge.

This organizational change, nay transformation, programme looks as if it could be a good opportunity to do something a bit different.

But you pause. You know how often many big organizational change programmes fail. Typically, all the focus, effort and energy ends up being on new structure charts, a scrabble for senior posts and a perceived fear for many of ending up with a bad manager, or worse ending up in the redeployment pool. Most staff are, therefore, unlikely to be on board with this change.

You also wonder who's going to lead this, as there's no obvious choice, no one you know of who has the skills and experience needed for delivering a large complex organizational change programme, especially one that's going to impact on pretty much the entire workforce.[1] It's highly likely, you think, that it will be given to someone who's about ready to retire but needs something to keep them busy for their last couple of years. The worst-case scenario would be to bring in consultants.

You recall an article you read recently about the Rank Group, who own Mecca Bingo. They transformed a huge chunk of their business from bingo halls and slot machines (buildings) to online bingo and gambling (apps). Key to delivering these transformed services required a complete overhaul (transformation) of the back office that ran and managed the services. They had to transform the general workforce, and this proved to be the biggest challenge.

So, while you're excited by the potential of this programme (because you're the optimistic sort and think maybe this time things will be different), you're also pretty sceptical that it will be approached as anything more than a rejig of the existing org chart.

But you're looking for a challenge and it will be great learning, so you volunteer. And after much delay (for this is an organization that likes to take its time in decision-making), you're called upon to lead on innovation.

And you, dear reader, yes you, have an opportunity right now to personally take on this challenge. Do you think you're up for it? If so, then let's get you ready.

---

[1] And by delivering you mean delivering the benefits and outcomes, not managing the process of the programme – many can do that but it's managing the impact and outcomes that's key to success.

First up. Some background.

No one in the organization really knows what innovation means. This has one advantage in that you can make it mean whatever you want it to mean. Within reason. The catch? Everyone else will want you to deliver what they think it means.

Personally, you think it's definitely not about shiny gadgets and upgraded software, which is what many are talking about, especially as there's a digital workstream that should pick all of this up.[2] Additionally, some of the programme aims are about staff and ways of working, such as an agile and empowered workforce, which will be needed to implement the digital solutions.

So, from your perspective the focus of innovation should be about ways of working and how we get things done. It's about innovating organizational frameworks, structures, cultures, skills, etc. that will allow change to be the norm and, therefore, easier to do. It's about working smarter not harder. Personally, you think procuring shiny gadgets is just that – procurement. They might be needed but shouldn't be the sole focus because if staff and process aren't

---

[2] Remember iPads… and how prolific they were for a while, how innovative everyone thought they were being as they started using them to get people to sign in at an office building or providing you with an extensive wine menu in a restaurant until realizing that the old paper process/version was actually a better system. Shiny gadgets without any thinking about how people will use them just become add-ons and can easily make things worse rather than better, while using up all the money needed for real change.

equipped and enabled to adopt and adapt these shiny gadgets that will 'transform' services, then the shiny gadgets will just end up collecting dust on the shelf.

Your key aim on this adventure is to explore how the organization works (people, process, skills) and how it needs to innovate in these areas to be able to transform the services it provides alongside becoming a great place to work and learn.

You also know top-down approaches don't work for this type of thing, especially when badged with terms such as 'culture change'. You therefore anticipate that you'll need a different way to communicate and engage with staff and teams across the organization. A bottom-up approach that maybe starts many fires burning in different areas to see what lands and what starts to spread is what you feel you and your team of zero will need to do. Yes, that's right. You don't have a team. It's just you. So you'll also need to find a crew to help you in this adventure. A crew you can lean on when times get tough. Because they will. Get tough.

Finally, there's no preset formula, process or off-the-shelf certificate for this, so you'll need to learn as you go how to become a Change Ninja.

How to play

Unlike many books on change – you know, the academic ones that tell you what you should do and where you're going wrong, often written by someone who's never actually worked as a small cog in a giant machine – this book is an adventure book where *you* get to decide what to do, and *you* get to experience first-hand what happens based on that decision. There will be battles, challenges and learning along the way, with some useful tools provided that will help you not only with this adventure but in life's real adventures too.[3]

You can measure how well you're doing by checking the lifelines and energy scores each decision brings. Just like many computer games, you'll start with three lives and 100% health. These appear throughout the book when decisions or actions are taken that can impact on your general energy ⊕ (health) and motivation ⓥ levels (lives). Reduced motivation will lose a life; time spent battling or doing pointless things will reduce your energy levels. Sometimes the battle or pointless activity is worth it for the longer game but

---

[3] Some of these challenges, in fact most, may relate to human blockers just doing their jobs. Remember, it's the systems and organizations, the culture, processes and hierarchies that dictate how and what we should do. The culture of 'this is how we do things' provides a legitimacy that convinces those working in an organization that they're doing the right thing.

only you can decide whether it's the right choice. If you lose too many lives, though, and don't have the motivation to do something about it, then I'm afraid it will be game over. But don't worry… you can start again.[4]

I've also generously supplied you with a rucksack full of things to help on your adventure. It contains tenacity bars, curiosity pills, keep-calm lozenges and reserve tonic. All required to keep you strong as you battle the beasts.

But, most important is a book called 'Sami's Fables'. Sami has a lot to share on things that can go wrong and tools to use so that you don't have to repeat the mistakes Sami makes in becoming a Change Ninja. Sami's Fables, just like Aesop's, all have some wise learning that should do you well for any other adventures you may embark on. And for real emergencies, you can also draw on a superhuman strength that pauses time and gives you time to think before you respond. But this is only for absolute emergencies so use it wisely.

Are you ready to begin?

---

[4] Or cheat by just going back to the last decision and choosing a different option. No one is watching!

Characters

Remember the characters you'll come across in the book are entirely fictional. But you'll recognize them because they're also generically common. They're everywhere. The main players are described here as a 'type'. This means you can make them who you need them to be and give them the names of who they might be in *your* story. But don't just think of them as goodies or baddies. If you try to understand their intent, it will help you make the right decisions.

You... yes you

You just want to get on and do a good job. Just like everyone else. But you also like to be challenged so seek out the new and untested. You don't really like rules, at least rules that make no sense. And you know you can't change things if you don't break a few rules. That is, after all, what they're there for. But you don't always get it right and you don't always act as you're expected to, so you need to remember to be careful and stay quiet *a lot*. Remember, not everyone likes a rule breaker, however small or ridiculous the rule.

The Big Cheese

Every organization has a chief executive. Most have the character trait of wanting to be in charge and wanting people to do what they want them to do. How they do this can be good, bad or indifferent, depending on their ego. Invariably, to get to this position you need to go on lots of leadership programmes at high-ranking institutes. The Big Cheese mostly makes decisions for what seems like the right reason. At times they can seem a little impatient and unapproachable but mostly their bark is definitely worse than their bite. They will, at times be helpful – just don't ask for help too often.

Mini Cheddars

These are the decision-making managers. In theory. On paper. They aspire to be a Big Cheese. Many aren't, however, Big Cheese material. Most of the ones in this adventure aren't Big Cheese material. They're lacking some of the key ingredients. This becomes apparent when they feel as if they don't have full control and start behaving badly to try to get control. They spend a lot of time finding ways to avoid making decisions. You'll need to hide your frustrations well when in meetings with the Mini Cheddars.

The Boss

We all have one. They can sometimes be a good boss and sometimes not. But good or bad here is all about perspective. They are, after all, human just like you and they also have a boss, who may be good or not. We'll just call the boss the Boss in this story. Your relationship with the Boss, managed well, can be symbiotic.

Eddie Obeng – The Prof

Eddie is the only real character. Brought into the organization by the Big Cheese for many of the right things, but often at the wrong time. Eddie knows a lot about change and transformation and shares many of his tools throughout the book. You don't meet the Prof straightaway, but you find out about him early from Sami, who mentions him a lot.[5] Use his teaching wisely on your adventure and you'll go far.

---

[5] Remember you have a copy of Sami's Fables to help you on your adventure.

The Steely Governance Manager

This person appears friendly and helpful but has a steely interior. They're like a walking clipboard, are very risk averse and like bureaucracy and detail. They don't like new things (too risky) and can often be heard saying, 'But that's not how we do things.' They like to imagine the worst-case scenario and only the worst-case scenario before saying you can't do something because 'worst-case scenario…' Be wary of going into battle with them.

The Digital Transformation Director

They've been appointed specifically to do all things digital and transformative. So, they're a bit younger and hipper than the regular IT directors. They don't sit behind a desk, that's old school, but like to sit round a low coffee table, hands behind their head and left foot resting on their right thigh. They were selected because of their experience in transformation (which they keep telling you about) and they're here to transform things. But all in good time. First, they plan to reorganize the department and all energy is on working out the new structure chart. You'll need to find ways to keep them on side.

Volunteers

They come in all shapes and sizes. Just people who want to do some good stuff. To learn new things. To make a bigger impact. Happy to do what's needed. Wanting to know more. Often fighting on the inside against the system and their managers, who are less keen on them doing 'other' things that aren't in their job description. Opposite of a 'jobsworth'. You just need to support them when needed and give lots of appreciation and recognition.

The Blockers

They say the right things when they need to (i.e. in front of others). They agree that change is needed, nay essential, *but...* they will stop you. Especially if it's not their idea. How dare you suggest things could be better/improved/different. Don't you know they're a manager, and this is their speciality? They're normally good schmoozers though. And very good at calmly providing *excuses* for not doing something while you turn into a rabid beast trying to point out that they're *blocking* progress. You need to be permanently on guard for them. They can easily snare you with their fake charm.

Jim

Jim is a generic middle manager. He tries hard. It's hard not to like him because he *means well*. Jim wants to be liked and likes everyone. He likes to make bad jokes and laugh at them. If you don't laugh back, he repeats them, assuming you didn't hear him. Jim is a pain in the arse. But he means well. A bit of flattery with Jim will get you far.

Maya

Maya is a bit like Jim. A generic middle manager. She's had to fight hard to be in this role and get to this level and she didn't do it by accepting fools graciously. Maya also means well. But her tone can be a little off. She can come across a little dismissive and finger pointy. Maya, like Jim, is a pain in the arse. But remember, she means well. Acknowledging how well Maya has done despite the system will get you far.

Pirates – your crew

These are the people you'll meet, gather, cry and laugh with. They, like you, break the rules for the right reasons, and they want to do good things so keep going like a dog with a bone. It's essential you gather a crew quickly, and you'll learn how to do this later. They're not your team or even your colleagues. They're a crew who will morph and change over time but you must gather a crew quickly.

Corridor of Gloom

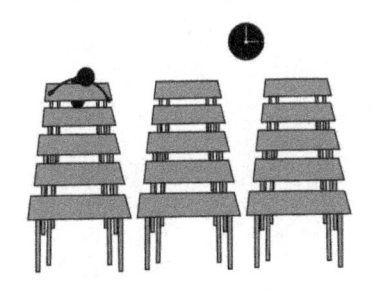

This is the office building you work in. One of those ugly, square, modern office buildings where everything nice has been removed to make space for rows and rows of desks. Where colour has been excluded (too much of a distraction) and everything is grey. The walls, the carpet, the blinds. Where the lights flicker and make noises and can't be switched off. Where the air con is either blasting cold air or blasting nothing. Everything is centrally controlled, so nowhere has the right light or temperature. Where it's both noisy and eerily quiet at the same time. Where the air is filled with emails going back and forth between people who could touch each other without moving if they stretched their arms out. Where there's a sea of cables on display emerging from the back of equipment. Where hot-desking is now a thing and, to make them easy to find, small images of flames are stuck on them. There are offices but only the Mini Cheddars get one of these. The offices are also grey. Square grey boxes in the middle of the Corridor of Gloom.

Challenge 1

Innovation workshop

⊘ 100 ⓸ 3

Your adventure begins on a gloomy Wednesday afternoon in February. You've been invited to a workshop to help define the new transformational organizational change programme. As is typical for many change programmes, the ambitions are high, the focus areas decided and each theme/stream has an identified lead who will now be known as 'Head of...' (you had a string of emails last week alerting you that some of these leads had already updated their LinkedIn profiles with their new position title).

As the new Head of Innovation, you're full of hope for this workshop because, as I mentioned at the start, you're the optimistic type and think this might be a real chance to make some real change happen. Perhaps now you'll find out *why* this programme is being run. What, in particular, is it that needs to change and why does the organization need to transform? While you're excited about being involved and think this will be a rewarding programme to be involved in, you're still sketchy about the problem that the programme is trying to solve.

You're also aware of the potential downside of this programme. The entire organization is about to be shaken upside down and inside out, with a majority of staff needing new job descriptions in new structures, with roles that they ultimately may need to apply for, and which may be at a different grade to their current one. While there are no redundancies, at least, there's still the looming threat for everyone of ending up in the dreaded redeployment zone. So, you imagine the problem statement that led to this programme must be nice and meaty and you're looking forward to hearing it in full, so you can start thinking about what particular challenge areas need some innovative thinking.

You walk into the cramped room that's been booked for the workshop. It's mostly full of furniture, and people are squeezing behind chairs to go and get a hot drink. Someone has pinned up the aims of the programme on recycled (grey) A3 paper and stuck them to the end wall. You can just about make them out.[6]

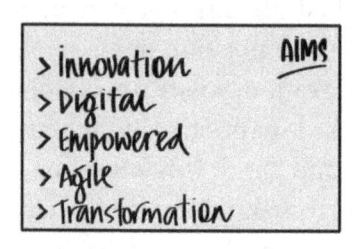

AIMS
> Innovation
> Digital
> Empowered
> Agile
> Transformation

The other three walls are covered with flipchart

---

[6] Including Innovation, Digital, Empowered, Agile, with an overall aim of Transformation.

paper with dates above for the next three years. It's a giant calendar. You note that each of the three facilitators are project managers. You know these people and they're very good project managers, especially when the task is clear and requires sticking to standard process, governance, developing Gantt charts and producing lots of documentation. But you're not entirely sure facilitation of such a workshop (where everything is still pretty vague – after all, the aims are just words and don't yet have any description of what success would look like) is their core strength. Especially as, looking around the room at who else is here, you imagine there will be a lot of 'opinions' that need managing and, well, facilitating. But you are, despite this, still feeling positive and optimistic, so smile at everyone as you say hello.

There's a brief introduction from one of the Mini Cheddars reminding everyone of the programme aims, which are to become more innovative, more digital, to empower staff, to be more agile and to ultimately transform the organization. But there's still no description of the problem to solve or what the transformed organization is expected to look like.

Why do we need to be more digital? you really want to ask, and *What's the real problem that digital will fix?* but you decide it's a bit early in the session to raise such thoughts as it would sound as if you were *already* questioning the purpose of the programme.

Everyone is then asked to grab a pen (a Sharpie no less) and some stickies and write down what each of you are planning to do in your specialist areas as the newly recruited 'Heads of'. You then need to say when you plan to do it by placing the activities on the giant calendar. 'This,' the facilitators/PMs say, 'will give us a three-year plan of what by when for the Exec team.'

You pause and think. You were only given this role a couple of weeks ago.[7] And this role is to lead on innovation. For the organization. To help it transform. This is all the detail you have, so what's being asked of you just now makes no sense. You wonder whether you've missed something and the others have more information than you do about the end goal and what it looks like but you're pretty sure they don't.

You sit back and try and summarize, in your head, where things are for you just now.

Innovation as a term for the organization hasn't really been defined. Which areas need innovation haven't been discussed. Who the target audience is for the innovative solutions hasn't been agreed.[8] *And there's no defined problem statement to guide us on what might need solving in an innovative way.*

You raise your hand and say, 'I'm finding this quite hard,' before repeating the thoughts that just went through your mind.

'Well, just do the best you can,' says one of the project managers. 'We need a plan to go back to the Exec team next week.'

---

[7] Or a few pages ago.
[8] Internal (staff) or external (customers)?

You swallow that feeling of here we go again re. death by project plan when the end point or intended outcomes haven't yet been defined.[9]

'Well, it's just that it would be really helpful to have a bit more discussion around the problems we're trying to fix so we could then focus on key areas we feel need innovative solutions. So, if that's not what this session is about then could we have a session that's about that? This would be my first suggested task to help define some target area, but beyond that I don't really know what we'll do at this stage.'

'No, we're not doing that today. Please just give it a go if you can. We need to create a programme plan. The Exec have insisted they get a 'what by when' for the next three years for next week's board meeting. It needs to cover all the themes and it's your job to do it for innovation.'

Well. That's you told…

You raise your hand again.

'Me again… I'm also struggling with developing a three-year plan for innovation in general. Shouldn't it be more iterative than descriptive, trial and error, changing as we learn, but in line with some key

---

[9] This might sound like you are anti project managers and programme offices when you're not. In fact, you used to be one and manage one. But you also recognize when the standard process of project management is not particularly helpful. When, for example, the end point or how to get there hasn't yet been defined but you still have to produce all the 'documentation' as it's good practice. Applying the standard process for these projects just turns everything into a bureaucratic exercise rather than something that can support and aid delivery of successful outcomes.

problem areas or intended outcomes? If we know what the solution is already, then I'd say it's probably not very innovative. As a suggestion could we maybe, if not discussing the problem we're trying to fix, spend some time looking at what we might look like once we've transformed, to give us a focus point?'

Eyes start rolling and sighs start sighing. The individuals in the room are used to 'this kind of behaviour' from you. Always asking your difficult questions and challenging the task rather than just getting on with doing what they want you to do.

'For goodness' sake,' replies one of the Mini Cheddars. 'Can you just put some things down that you might innovate and when you might innovate them.'

Current status ☻ 78 ☻ 3

Decision time

Do you:

a) Think, *I'll add some things and change them later to keep the peace*? (page 21)
or
b) Start to feel a bit frustrated, as this isn't what you signed up for? (page 25)

Before you make a decision, remember this is an adventure game where you get to decide what you'd do next. So, think carefully about the decisions before making a move as each decision will impact on your health and lifelines.

Think I'll add some things and change them later to keep the peace

You know that if you add things now it's possible it will get signed off and you'll be expected to then report on it every month. And all you've got are ideas for a few improvement projects that are already under way. If you add them, you'll have committed to half-heartedly supporting them and you know they'll likely never complete, and even if they do, they won't improve much. That's why you were excited by this big change programme. You thought it would stop these half-hearted change projects running, which use all the resources and energy and deliver little in terms of outcomes.

But it's the easy step, so you do it.

Current status ⏱ 55 ◐ 2

After you've done it and the plan is being summarized and read back you realize you've made the first step to giving up. You know people who've given up. They still have the same job and come into work every day with the same complaints and grumbles. And you've always wondered why they don't do something about it. You've heard stories about how great they used to be until the system wore them down. And now it's just a job that pays the wages and will hopefully pay a pension.[10] They seem to get little satisfaction from what they're doing and are just waiting to retire. Is this where you're headed? Will you be happy just going along with everyone, pretending, never questioning, and filling your days with pointless and futile activities?

Current status ⏲ 37 ◐1

You can stay quiet (keep reading) or create a time machine and wind back an hour and choose a different option (page 25).

---

[10] Commonly known as the golden handcuffs. A job that's hard to be forced from, an okay salary and a good pension. But a job that sucks the soul from you bit by bit, day by day.

Game over

You made a choice, you thought about it and stuck with it. And it may just be the right choice for you at this point in time. We all have different goals and aims in life. Different things we want to put our energy into. Different jobs we might want to do or organizations we might want to work in. We know when it's the right time to accept that a particular adventure is over and it's time to try something different.

But it wasn't the right choice for this particular adventure as you've run out of health and lives before reaching the end and possibly have wasted your money on this book.

Current status 🕐 0 🍎 0

Second chance

However... we all make mistakes or sometimes wish we'd made a different decision after the event, so if you've ended up here by mistake or changed your mind and would like to continue the journey, you can start again (or just go back to your previous decision and decide more wisely).

Start to feel a bit frustrated, as this isn't what you signed up for

Current status 🕐 57 💬3

You're losing energy. This time you really thought they meant that things were going to be done differently. When the Big Cheese and Execs had communicated the change programme you got a sense that they were really invested in it and would therefore make sure it wouldn't be the same old same old approach. But looking at what's going on the wall it seems everyone is happy to just reword the things they're already doing, a rebrand of current plans with the new aims added. Nothing. Transformative. At all.

You also know you can't properly articulate what your problem with the task is, especially as no one has really heard any of the things you've said so far. You're starting to doubt yourself and wonder whether maybe it's you that's got it all wrong. Did you miss something or misunderstand something? Why is it just you that seems to be struggling? An idea comes into your head. *I'll just try one last thing*, you think, *and try to get my point across with humour.*

You grab some stickies and scribble 'invent the time machine' and 'realize the time machine didn't work' and place them on the calendar at different dates. Yes, you know a time machine is more invention than innovation but how else are you meant to predict an undefined future when nobody, and I mean nobody, has yet to give you any idea of what the future needs to look like, whose future needs to change and what the problem is that means the future needs to be different.

Sadly, the point is entirely lost on everyone. It's assumed you're just being awkward, and the project managers are frustrated that you haven't put much of anything real on the plan beyond having an exploratory workshop and creative problem-solving session.

One of the Mini Cheddars takes you aside at the end of the meeting and 'has a word' about your lack of cooperation and how disappointed they are in your behaviour. You try again to share your concerns around it being too vague and needing proper exploration, in collaboration with stakeholders, but they tell you, 'It's your job to work it out and come back with the answers and a what by when by the end of the week. Please.'

Reflecting later you acknowledge that your attempt at humour to make a point wasn't particularly clever but it really did give you insight into how big a challenge the whole thing is going to be. But how to avoid all this unnecessary process to stop it becoming yet another big exercise of long meetings, paper writing, bureaucracy and governance that will suck the life out of everyone while delivering very little?

Aha, you think. *Maybe this is the insight I was after. Maybe this is where the real innovation is needed.* Maybe this was the problem statement you were after all along. You know that no one else sees it this way (yet) but it gives you firm resolve to have a jolly good crack at trying to do something innovative about it.

Current status ☻ 75 ☻ 3

This is your first learning curve. You know that things weren't right, but you don't yet have the right tools and language to articulate it properly. It's early in the journey and you know there's a lot of learning ahead, but you wonder whether that book in your rucksack, Sami's Fables, would be of use right now. You reach in and pull it out, settling down to read the first tale.

Sami's Fables Part 1

The professor of change

Sami was in trouble again. Sami had been asked to do something for a project but didn't know how because it didn't make sense. Sami had been asked to provide a project plan and a business case for a piece of work that was incredibly vague and had no clear expectation of what was needed, but there was a burning platform to do something.[11] Sami's boss reminded Sami that they were smart and therefore could only assume that Sami was being difficult by not doing what was being asked.

'We have a process,' stated Sami's boss, 'for managing projects, so please will you just follow it.'

So, Sami did the only thing Sami could think of doing because Sami knew the process was the wrong process for what was needed. Sami phoned a friend and reached out to Prof. Eddie Obeng for help.[12] The

---

[11] Well, smouldering, maybe.
[12] Remember, he's actually real. You can look him up if you don't believe me. You'll meet him yourself later in the journey.

Prof listened to Sami's complaints then explained why Sami was struggling so much.[13]

'You need to know about the types of change,' the Prof said. 'If you identify the type of change you're doing before you start, you'll then know what process to follow rather than blindly assuming it will be exactly like the last project you worked on. Only then can you manage change effectively. And before I explain them you should know that most organizations use the same process regardless of the type of change and that's what you're now up against.'

The Prof then went on to describe these types of change in more detail:

'Firstly, there's Paint by Numbers. Remember those paint by numbers sets you used to get as a kid? There was always a mad aunt who thought you'd enjoy them. They came with all the instructions of what to do so you *knew how* to do it, and you had a very clear picture of *what* you were trying to achieve, often a picture of a horse. Even if the following year's set was a picture of a different horse, the process was the same each time. So, when you have a change type

---

[13] But only for a few minutes which the Prof felt was more than adequate time for complaining.

where you *know what* you're doing and *know how* to do it, it's called Paint by Numbers, or PbN. You can plan them out in detail, write a solid business case that will likely be okay and not expect too many surprises along the way.'

The Prof continued with the next description:

'Secondly comes Movies. Have you ever tried to make a funny video, one of those you can submit to TV shows to win £200? If you have, you know they're hard to do. You may know how to go about doing it. You have a camera, sound, lighting and editing equipment but you often don't know what the what is until the end when you play back all your takes, carefully edit them and find they're still not funny. This type of change, when you *know how* but *don't know what* is called a Movie project.

'Are you still with me?' the Prof asked Sami.

Sami responded in the affirmative before saying, 'But I don't think my project meets either of those descriptions.'

'No, that's coming,' replied the Prof before carrying on.

'Next comes Quests. Remember King Arthur? If not, here's a reminder. King Arthur had a goal and that was to find the Holy Grail. But he had no idea how to go about finding it. Can you imagine writing a business case and three-year plan for a goal you don't know how to achieve?[14] But King Arthur was smart, so he gathered his knights, shared his vision (to find the Holy Grail), gave them a sack of gold and a time limit and sent them off to different parts of the world to try to find the treasure. "Report back in exactly three months," was his parting instruction. Three months later the knights reported back. They all reassessed what they should do next and where they should search next before heading off again. A project when you *know what* but *don't know how* (you've never done this type of change before) is a Quest. Many of the changes in organizations today are Quests. They might have clear goals but getting there is still unknown territory. Like King Arthur, you need to do it in chunks, learn from what you find, before deciding and doing the next chunk.'

The Prof was talking fast and drew breath before saying, 'And finally…

'Fog. Have you ever been in a group caught on a hillside and the fog has come down? You get cold, it's damp, it's dark and you're scared. You know you can't just stay where you are, but you don't know what to do or how to do it. If you just march off, you may become lost or fall off a cliff. So, you tie yourselves together and take very small iterative steps, checking

---

[14] Sami could, as that's exactly what Sami had been asked to do.

for clues as you go. Can you hear water? Which way is it flowing? When you *don't know what* to do and *don't know how* to do it, but know you can't stay where you are, you're dealing with a Foggy project. Transformation and innovation programmes at the start are often foggy. Your organization needs to transform, but you don't yet have a clear view of what that transformation looks like or how to go about it. However, you know that if you do nothing the organization might fail. Sometimes these types of change will eventually become Quests, with more clarity over the end point, the what, as you take your small steps and keep reassessing, but the how is still unknown because you've never done this type of change before.'

The Prof continued:

'Only once you've identified the type of change can you really understand what process you need to deliver it. If you're used to doing long three-year project plans and try to do that on a Foggy change type, you're likely to fail. Remember, very small exploratory steps are needed to stop you falling off a hidden cliff edge.[15]

---

[15] If you know about PRINCE2 methods for projects, this is a good process for PbN projects but useless for Foggy projects. If you know about agile methods and sprints, then this is a good process for a Quest – short sprints and retrospectives just like King Arthur. If you're not familiar with either (and even if you are) you can't go wrong with Prof. Eddie Obeng's *All Change!*, which provides the process for each type in more detail.

'You also need to think about leadership and the team. Some leaders love Painting by Numbers. They like the clarity and lack of surprise. This sounds like some of the people you've mentioned. They just want a what by when and some assurance it will happen. Foggy projects make them anxious and nervous, so they try to turn them into a PbN and then become frustrated when you can't make that happen. But others love a Fog or a Quest and become bored by PbN projects. They'll likely cause havoc trying to make it more creative and exciting. Everyone has a preference. There's no right and wrong answer but knowing your preference and those of your teams is massively helpful. If you're in the Fog and love being in the Fog but your team prefers PbN, then you need to lead them in a way that will reduce their anxiety and stress.[16]

'So, Sami?' asked the Prof, 'what type of change do you think you have?'

'A Quest,' responded Sami immediately. 'And now I can explain this to my boss so we can hopefully approach it differently.'

'Great,' replied the Prof. 'We'll make a Change Ninja of you before you know it. Got to go,' and he put the phone down.

---

[16] You can do this by making the small iterative steps very small PbN chunks of change. The same works for Quests too.

Sami wasn't at all sure what this Change Ninja reference was about but was delighted with the learning.

Ninja moves

> ### There's more than one way
>
> Before you start any change, however small, work out what type of change it is. Then ask yourself: 'How do I feel?' about this type of change. Is it a preference or outside your comfort zone? What are the behaviours and actions needed to lead this type of change? And what might you need to work on to lead the change effectively?
>
> Next, think about the team you're leading. What do the individual team members feel about this type of change? What type of leadership do they need to ensure they can deliver what's needed? Are they anxious or bored? How will you manage this?
>
> And whatever you do, don't try to follow a PbN process when you're lost in the fog. You'll fall off the cliff. You can tell your boss this the next time they ask for a three-year project plan for a vague type of change. But use the stories to tell them rather than just telling them they're wrong. That way they'll reach their own conclusions and get their own insights.

> Many of today's organizational objectives are foggy. Ask yourself whether anyone really knows what 'digital transformation' really means? But many will use big words to make it sound like they know what it's all about. However, they're just that… big words. Don't be fooled. But do work out with your team or colleagues what type of change it is so you can use the right process to progress, at least to the next decision point and avoid falling off the cliff edge.

Tools and templates

Types of change

Not all projects or change activities are the same types of change. I repeat, not all projects or change activities are the same type of change. Ask yourself:

a) Do you know how to do it? (i.e. you've done something very similar before)

and

b) Do you know what to do? (i.e. the end objective or goal is very clear, something you can describe with clarity)

If the answer is no to both, then a standard project management process such as PRINCE2 won't help you. It will only make life very difficult. By knowing the type of change you're leading you can identify the appropriate process you need to use to help you manage it more effectively. Use the 'Types of Change' grid to decide what type of change you're trying to do. Do this with the team so everyone is clear about the projects you're working on.

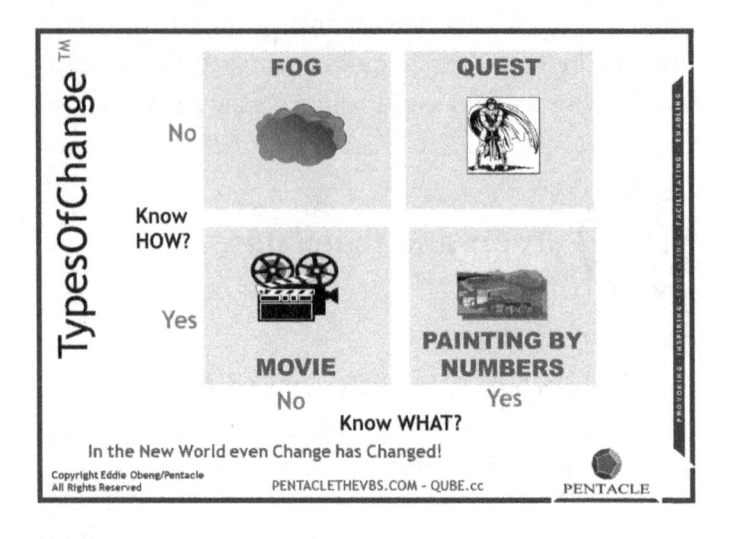

TypesOfChange™

	Know WHAT? No	Know WHAT? Yes
Know HOW? No	FOG	QUEST
Know HOW? Yes	MOVIE	PAINTING BY NUMBERS

In the New World even Change has Changed!
Copyright Eddie Obeng/Pentacle
All Rights Reserved
PENTACLETHEVBS.COM - QUBE.cc
PENTACLE

Your reflection

You put Sami's Fables down and sit back and think.

It would have been really helpful to know this *before* that workshop, but better late than never.

You think about your vague objectives and the overall programme of change. You work in an area (health) where demand outstrips supply and costs are increasing exponentially (but resource doesn't), therefore you could safely assume that this is ultimately the pressing need/burning platform problem that requires a big change programme.

Having better clarity about the types of change could have helped you explain why you were struggling (the programme was clearly still quite foggy, particularly for innovation) and as a team you needed to explore the overall desired outcomes more to try to turn it into a Quest. They were clearly used to running PbN projects and were trying to do the same with this change programme. Using their known (standard) methods and tools because that's all they knew. And because they didn't know about the other change types, they didn't realize that this was the wrong process.

But you didn't yet have this knowledge during that initial workshop to be able to articulate this properly. And neither did the organization.

Just reading this and knowing where you went wrong and how you'll approach this type of challenge in the future has boosted your health by 15 points. If only that time machine had worked, you could go back to before the workshop and start all over.

☗ + 15

Challenge 2

Creating space

Current status 🕐 90 ♥ 3

You head into work and feel like you're walking into a Victorian matchstick factory. The open plan Corridor of Gloom with its row upon row of office desks, with its grey walls and grey carpet. The Mini Cheddars' offices run down the middle of the grey space,[17] casting unnatural light into the corridor.[18] Outside the sun is shining so those lucky to have window seats have pulled down the grey blinds

---

[17] For they're senior managers and therefore exempt from the open plan 'it's good for collaboration' policy.

[18] Well, that's until there's no (or little) movement in the offices, at which point the lights automatically switch off. This can be quite entertaining as it's common for managers to start whizzing about on their chair and waving their arms in the air to reactivate the lights. They pretty much always whizz about on their chairs, even though it would be *much* easier to just stand up and walk to the door and back.

Challenge 2: Creating space

to block it out. Everyone is sitting in rows, heads down, headphones on, busy tap tap tapping out emails to people sitting two metres away. There's a hushed library silence. A rogue laugh creates a collaborative frown. Did I mention it's grey?

Recently you've been reading a lot about creativity, particularly about creating the right environments to encourage creativity. Glancing around at the 20 shades of grey you wonder whether this is something you need to explore more for the office. Creative, inspiring and colourful spaces with tools, digital whiteboards, bean bags, table tennis… is it gimmicky? Probably yes. But there needs to be something, somewhere people are allowed, nay encouraged, to go, to collaborate, think, draw out ideas, make noise, laugh even.

If there's nowhere that people can go to think about things, and also a perception that there's 'no permission', then it's unlikely you'll get the collaborations, creativity, innovations and adoption that you seek.[19]

Something needs to change at this most basic level but you're not sure where to start.

You walk around the building looking for inspiration and ideas. As you go, you keep looking out the window. There's an unused and unloved outdoor space. *Mmmmm…*, you think, *I wonder whether we could get a budget for a big eco hut*. You instantly know the answer will be no. But what else? What might sit more

---

[19] There's a strong culture of presenteeism, and if you're not at your desk, then you must be skiving.

comfortably? An idea you can 'sandwich' between doing nothing and the eco hut.[20]

And then you stumble on an empty corner tucked away. This, you think, could be a start, a creative corner. You check with facilities. There are no immediate plans for the space, so you ask for temporary use and put the idea to the Boss.[21] As you expected, they agree to you using the empty corner as a creative space (although you're pretty sure they were *almost* tempted to pursue the eco hut idea).

You put out a call for help and gather those that answered in the space and explain about having some space that would help creative thinking, be informal and a drop-in area for sharing ideas. You also emphasize the lack of any real budget.

'So, how can we use this out-of-the-way grey space for something useful? How might we create a creative space that encourages broader thinking and collaborative working? How will we draw people in? How shall we make it look different?'

A plan emerges. Fake grass is suggested. A colleague suggests her husband could donate it from his company. 'Cowhide bean bags too,' says someone else. The team

---

[20] Basic options in any business case: do nothing, do something amazing but possibly high-cost/high-risk, or do something in the middle that sits more comfortably with everyone. The middle solution (and mostly the one you've already decided is the best option) is normally the compromise solution everyone agrees on, and therefore everyone gets what they want.

[21] Empowering staff is still some way off. *Everything* needs signing off by someone more senior, irrelevant of personal rank.

Challenge 2: Creating space

members are enthused and excited and volunteer for actions.

Three days later, while you're working at home, two back-to-back calls come.

The first is from the Steely Governance Manager, who's heard about your plans for the space, imagined the worst possible scenario and decides it's too high-risk... Imagine if the press found out(?)... Waste of taxpayers' money(?)... Reputational risk(?)... etc. etc., and she says she's closing the entire idea down.

Before you have time to process this, the phone rings again. It's your colleague in charge of the fake grass and cowhide bean bags. You can hear panic in her voice. It transpires that the grass has arrived and been left in front of reception. The problem? Well, a) there's a lot of it, and b) it's not fake.

'What do you want to do about it?' she asks.

'Well,' you say, 'I think you should be really, really careful when ordering the cowhide bean bags.'[22]

Current status ⏱ 68 ◐ 2

---

[22] And once you've stopped laughing suggest she asks whether anyone is remodelling their garden and donating the mound of turf, as long as they can take it away today. It's thankfully quickly snapped up as reception staff were *not* happy at the instant welcoming lawn at the front door.

Decision time

Do you:

a) Fight, literally, for your (creative) corner? (page 42)

or

b) Decide this is a battle not worth the effort? (page 43)

Before you decide, a word of caution

Some battles are worth fighting for. Some battles you really want to win. Battles you'll put all of your energy into. But remember, battles burn up lots of energy (check your health score) and eat away at your resilience (check your life score). Battles are also frustrating and sometimes pretty pointless. Battles can be lost. And even when you win you may still not get the results you hoped for.

So, what decision will you make: a) or b)?

Fight, literally, for your (creative) corner

It's the following day and you go into battle. You knock on the Steely Governance Manager's door and ask for five minutes. They're sat behind their desk. A barrier before you've even started. Reluctantly they invite you to sit down. You start explaining your problem and why you're frustrated but it's not very coherent and sounds like a rant.[23]

---
[23] Which it is.

Current status ⊙ 25 ◐ 2

Halfway through, you wonder, *Was the creative corner really that good an idea?* You can already see it isn't that well thought through and the anticipated outcome vs effort is unlikely to make it worthwhile. The eco hut on the other hand… now that *was* a good idea.

If you do think this fight is worth continuing with, I suggest you jump to page 106, where you'll find a useful tool called IDQB™ to help with this type of challenge. Doing so will at least boost your energy levels (by +30 points) before you head into the battle. And you'll need all the energy you can get.

It's not too late to change your mind though. If you want to step back from this go to page 42 and choose again. Or if you've simply just had enough already. Why bother? No one else does. Go straight to page 23. Do not pass go, do not collect £200 and do not press the reset button.

Decide this is a battle not worth the effort

You decide this isn't the battle to try to make a big stance over. Realistically, you know it wasn't really going to deliver on its promises, it was too homemade, not well thought through, there was no senior support, no budget to make it a real thing and it would need a lot of managing for probably little gain. Early in this journey you begin to recognize when you need to give in, learn (smart failure) and move on… you gather the team in the non-creative grey corner and start thinking again.

Current status 🕐 57 ⓘ 2

And after lots of chat with the volunteers some new ideas emerge (which you'll subsequently deliver), including:

Friday film club in the canteen

Ingredients:

1 x TED talk

1 x host (ideally a senior, well-known [liked], manager)

Many bags of popcorn

Method:

Create posters to advertise the events, run the film on a big screen in the canteen, invite the host to run the Q&A. Run at all office locations, rotating films as you go.

Randomized coffee trials

Ingredients:

Voluntary sign-up process

1 x co-ordinator

Method:

Create posters, invite people to sign up, randomly match them to two other people and connect them, suggesting they arrange to meet for coffee and share whatever they'd like to share and feed back what happened.

Challenge 2: Creating space

Both are quick to set up, are low-cost, build skills in the volunteers who manage the process and are new ways for staff across the organization to make new (random) connections, share knowledge and skills, find areas beyond their teams where they can support or become involved and get away from their desk. They support learning in different (diverse) and informal ways while being engaging.

Warning: You're asked whether the cost of the coffee can be claimed as an expense. You decide that this is a firm no. The coffee is obviously optional, and people need to want to do it – not be paid 'extra' to do it.

The response rate and feedback from both sets of events is hugely positive. You feel like you've finally made a start in getting people mobilized to do things a little bit differently.

Current status ☺ 82 ◐ 3

You reflect on your learning so far from these two challenges. There's the leaders and project managers all working as if the overall programme is a Paint by Numbers type of change. They're having lots of meetings, creating lots of documentation, having lots of discussion but not much else is happening. And then there's your new and evolving approach, which is tiny iterative steps of trial and error and learning as you go. There's still no clear path for innovation, but you're okay with this just now.

Your approach feels right but it needs bigger reach. You need to find others who recognize they too are in the fog and want to join up by a rope so you can all get out safely. You hoped the creative space might have helped with this, but you had to let it go. How else might you find these other people caught in the fog? You decide to see whether Sami's Fables has anything to share that might be useful.

Sami's Fables Part 2

Ship ahoy, me hearties

Sami had been trying to get people working more collaboratively on innovation for a while. Everyone seemed to be saying the same things, Sami thought.

Everyone complained about the same things, such as lack of resources, poor leadership, lack of consistency, and the worst one ever, silo working. This all drove Sami mad. None of it really described any real problems and everyone assumed that there was nothing they could personally do about it and that someone else would sort it out for them even though there was nothing obvious to sort out. Sami sometimes challenged this thinking by asking, 'So what do you do to break down silo working? What departments do you need to collaborate with that you don't collaborate with just now?'

'That's not my job,' was often the answer.

Everyone seemed to know what the problems were *and* what the solutions were, yet no one seemed willing to step up and just sort it out. Collectively. Together.

But there were also, Sami knew, people out there trying to really change things. People who were saying what sounded like the right things. Collaboration, creative problem-solving, trying new ways of working. But how to bring them together and create a network that could then deliver some outcomes?

Sami tried a couple of times, but it didn't stick. Those invited were initially excited but quickly went back to being busy at their day jobs when they realized this might be hard work. The excuse was that they had no time and this type of thing was a luxury they couldn't afford.[24]

Then Sami came across a book called *Be More Pirate*, which had rules for creating, well, a pirate crew.[25] Pirates, it seemed, weren't as bad as you might have previously imagined. Pirates came about to escape the tyranny and slavery of the Royal Navy. Pirate crews were democratic (they voted on who was to be captain), they had equality and diversity, no hierarchy, health insurance, and agreed shares of the booty. Pirate crews developed their own rules and

---

[24] Even though digital, innovation, culture and transformation were in every strategy, business plan and organizational message across the land.
[25] See reading recommendations at the end of the book for more information on two very useful resources. *Be More Pirate*, which is all about pirates, and *How to Be More Pirate*, which is all about modern-day tales of pirate activity for good. Both are inspirational, motivational and will give you even more ideas.

punishments. Pirate crews supported each other on common goals and for equal rewards.

Sami decided to try again, to build a crew. Reaching out in different places. Looking for people who might be pirates (rather than just wanting to wear the innovation badge because it sounded good). And creating a code with this group of how they would work resulted in much better success. Even when it was hard, the group supported and motivated each other and kept going. And this was what Sami needed. A like-minded crew.

Ninja moves

Find a crew

You need friends in many places. People who understand how hard it will be, who can support, mentor and motivate when it gets tough. And for whom you can do the same. A crew is likely made up of random pirates from all different places, often working on their own objectives and challenges but you'll be aligned on a common goal such as 'changing ways of working'. And your challenges will be made much easier if you can deal with them together. Sharing your knowledge and experience will help with delivery, moral support and

> courage to challenge when challenge is needed. You'll find you spend less time scratching your head and asking 'is it just me?' And you'll have somewhere to go when it all gets a bit too hard and you're tempted to give up. It will get hard but don't give up. Just 'Be More Pirate'.

Tools and templates

In the same boat

How often do you start a new project asking the team, 'What do we think this is all about?' or 'How do you think this should work?' before you start writing a project brief, communication or overview of what it is. Are you more likely to start with a draft paper for something before seeking opinions and comments from the wider team on what you've written?

To get alignment on a new activity (be it a project or about agreeing what this pirate crew are here to do) try using a 5Ps™ to

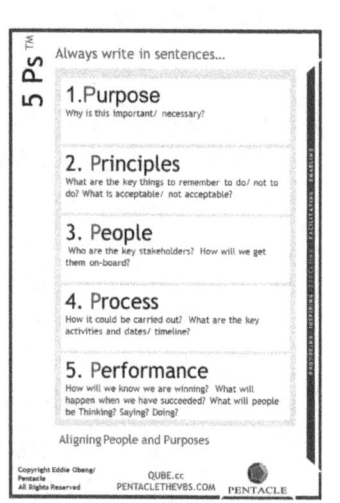

5 Ps™

Always write in sentences...

1. Purpose
Why is this important/ necessary?

2. Principles
What are the key things to remember to do/ not to do? What is acceptable/ not acceptable?

3. People
Who are the key stakeholders? How will we get them on-board?

4. Process
How it could be carried out? What are the key activities and dates/ timeline?

5. Performance
How will we know we are winning? What will happen when we have succeeded? What will people be Thinking? Saying? Doing?

Aligning People and Purposes

Copyright Eddie Obeng/ Pentacle
All Rights Reserved
QUBE.cc
PENTACLETHEVBS.COM PENTACLE

capture what everyone else thinks this activity is for and, most importantly, what success looks like:
- **Purpose**
- **Principles**
- **People** (stakeholders)
- **Process**
- **Performance**

Give the team five to ten minutes to write their responses on stickies to each of the 5Ps™ for the project or change activity. Do it without speaking. Once everyone is finished move the stickies about to inform a narrative and read it out loud. This way you'll get a wide range of input and varied views rather than just those of the loudest and most outspoken members of the team. Check in with everyone one by one to make sure they're happy with the content. Within 15 minutes you'll have a change brief that everyone agrees with, everyone understands, and a very clear idea of what success looks like.

Your reflection

You put the book down and realize the environment you need to create isn't physical. It's about people. You need to create the right working environment by having the right people in it. Only then will you create the environment to support creativity and problem-solving. You don't even need to physically meet, which means you can search beyond your local geography for the right people. You just need individuals who will stick at it, provide support when needed and some basic rules for working together.

You switch your laptop on and add *Be More Pirate* to your shopping basket.

Challenge 3

I didn't sign up for this

The big change programme is now under way and, as you predicted, not everyone is happy. There still seems to be a lot of uncertainty about things such as what jobs people will end up with and who their boss might be, and the benefits of all this change are still extremely vague.

Also, it's still being run as a Paint by Numbers project even though, while there might be some loosely described goals to aim for, no one really knows *how* it should be delivered. So you keep having to fill in paperwork that makes no sense.[26] You even have a KPI

---

[26] Remember, PbN projects are where you know what to do and know how to do it. Likely something you've done before.

to report on for innovation despite your protestations at the pointlessness of it.[27] And big buzzword bingo is in full swing at programme meetings.

But you at least have started to understand what some of the innovation goals need to be in relation to changing working practice, internal process and behaviours. Essentially, the people stuff. But the *how* is still very unclear as no one has done this before, at least in this organization and on this scale.

At the next programme board meeting, the Big Cheese makes an appearance and barks, 'We need to build some kind of award programme. Why don't we have one already? Wasn't someone already working on that? I'm sure we asked for this two years ago. Why didn't it happen?'[28]

Now, you're one of those types of people who can just get on with a bunch of random things and run with it. In the past you've been quite proud of this ability. *But...* as a result, you often get handed things that need doing and need doing now. Things that have often been 'hanging' around for a while, things that someone somewhere has failed to deliver.

---

[27] The KPI is for the number of 'ideas' the organization has every month, with an arbitrary target of 20. You did point out you had this many ideas most days while eating breakfast but were ignored and told to 'just get on with it'. The only upside is this means it's always green and you don't have to ask anyone for data. Nobody ever asks what your ideas are nor how good they are.

[28] It's worth noting that the Big Cheese's bark can be much much worse than their bite.

Challenge 3: I didn't sign up for this

So, you pretty much know what's coming when the Boss asks, 'Do you have five minutes? There's a little piece of work I'd like you to pick up.'

It transpires that a team has been working on a 'staff reward and recognition' programme for two years and has yet to deliver. No one, it seems, can agree on what it is that needs to be done,[29] and there has been a lot of 'discussion' about what would be an acceptable solution.[30] And now you're being asked to pick this up. And it needs to be delivered asap. It's not in your workstream or one of your objectives. Nor is it an interesting challenge *but* it is something you know you can pretty much do with your eyes shut even if it seems vastly unfair and even it feels like you're being punished for good behaviour.

Current status ☺ 78 ◐ 3

Decision time

Do you:

a) Put your foot down and say no – you already have more than enough work? (page 56)

or

b) Accept the challenge and figure you'll find a way to make it more interesting? (page 57)

---

[29] Sound familiar?

[30] To be fair to those involved, this piece of work needed to be managed as a project and it needed senior guidance and decision-making but instead it had been given to an operational team to lead and lacked seniors willing to make any decisions.

Put your foot down and say no

Why me? you think. You're busier than ever and are continuously delivering and going the extra mile. There was a team working on this for two years and you'll have to try to find a team (more volunteers, as you have no formal access to resources). Where's the accountability? The responsibility? How can people just get away with not delivering? You also know the department who failed to deliver will *not* be happy as it will be seen as stepping on toes rather than helping it.

No no no. It's not fair!

You don't say all this out loud, of course, but you do say you don't know how you can fit it in with an already busy schedule and that you know the other department won't be happy. But the Boss knows what you're really thinking. You can tell by the way they're looking at you.

Current status ☉ 47 ◐ 2

As you leave the room, you wonder whether you've made the right choice but head off to your next meeting, putting it to one side.

In the car on the way home you veer slightly into the hard shoulder as you realize your error. This was a golden opportunity to score major brownie points. And you could have done it without blinking. Instead, you huffed and you puffed and you blew your own house down.

Current status ☉ 14 ◐ 1

Should you go back tomorrow, apologize and say you were having a rough day and of course you'll do it (go to page 55 for a rewind of time and choose a different option – it will save you the apology)[31] *or* stick to your guns (go to page 23)?

Accept the challenge and figure you'll find a way to make it more interesting

You reflect. It's unfair. But it's the kind of project you can do with your eyes shut. You can use it to upskill a volunteer team. And, more importantly, you can use this to barter with the Boss when they next think of saying no to one of your crazy, nay creative, ideas. You recognize they've volunteered to take this on because they'll get brownie points for delivering. So, you too can use this for leverage in the future.

So, you accept.

You manage to gather a team to work on this and together produce some quick ideas (Thank You cards for managers to issue, Doing Something Different mugs for people who've tried new things). With some clever branding that aligns to the organization values you put these activities in place by the end of the month.

In parallel, you start to establish an annual awards programme. It's hard to make it interesting (there's too little challenge for you, it's a PbN project) but you decide to introduce a less obvious category for the awards called 'Smart Failure' for which individuals will self-nominate. This will help those who try to do

---

[31] That time machine seems to work after all.

things that don't always work get some recognition. It will also give you an idea of where the creative triers in the organization are. The Boss isn't convinced but you insist. They can hardly say no.

Current status ⏱ 72 ◐ 3

It's the day of the awards event. The guest compere is doing a great job and everyone seems happy to be there. About halfway through, the award for innovation is called out. You were excluded from seeing the nominations for this one so secretly think you may be shortlisted and even in with a chance of winning. You are, after all, Head of Innovation.

It turns out that you weren't even nominated, never mind shortlisted.

Current status ⏱ 52 ◐ 2

Next up is the self-nomination award for the smart failure. This one you win. It seems that no one else self-nominated. You've simultaneously won (the award) and failed (in getting others to share their ideas that didn't work).

Current status ⏱ 37 ◐ 2

But, overall, the event is a huge success and staff in attendance are all delighted to be there. You delivered the project in record time, over 200 Thank You cards have already been issued and you see the branded mugs being used around the building by those who've been gifted them. The Boss, the Big Cheese and Mini Cheddars are happy, and some staff have been recognized for their efforts and achievements.

It wasn't your ideal project, but you have a bunch of brownie points stored up, introduced the concept of smart failure and raised your profile with some senior managers. And it may just be your imagination, but some staff seem to be talking a little more positively about some of the big organizational changes that are being proposed.

Current status ⊙ 84 ⊙ 3

You're doing well. You've succeeded in the first three challenges and still have three lives, a lot of energy and you're starting to make some progress. But you've been working hard and it's a good time to take a break. Grab a cup of tea and a snack, and let's get back to Sami's Fables for some fresh insight.

Sami's Fables Part 3

Do your homework

Sami noticed that a lot of people were looking out the window and then noticed what sounded like people chanting. Sami headed over to the window to see what was going on.

In the overly full car park outside, there was a small crowd gathering around the mass of double-parked cars.[32] They were chanting what sounded like a demand, although the words were unclear. Someone from reception went out to speak to what looked like the ringleader but then quickly rushed back in.

The Mini Cheddars were curiously absent, and their rooms were in darkness. It was highly likely they were just sitting very still to avoid activating the lights in the hope that everyone would assume they weren't in.

Sami turned back to the window, and everyone was pointing and laughing at the giant inflatable rat

---

[32] There had been a raft of very angry emails from reception requesting people move their double-parked cars. Or else…

being held up by two of the protesters. It must have been a good ten metres high. There were also a few banners for one of the smaller unions.

They'll send in Ali, thought Sami. Ali wasn't yet a Mini Cheddar but was the recognized peacemaker and safe pair of hands, the safe compere, the one whose humour was deemed acceptable for any occasion. No one could not like Ali, so Ali was often rolled out on occasions like this. And then, as if by magic, Ali appeared in front of reception and asked to speak to the ringleader.[33] After a few minutes, Ali headed back inside and the protesters stopped chanting, turned around and headed back out of the gates. They looked both defeated and deflated. Even the giant inflatable rat had lost some air and was almost doubled over. Doubly deflated.

Everyone went back to their desk.

It transpired that the group had arrived with a letter of complaint they wanted to hand deliver to one of the head honchos. The only problem was that they'd got the wrong organization and the wrong office location.

---

[33] Much like the shopkeeper in *Mr Ben* cartoons.

Sami recalled the Prof saying 'never surprise your stakeholders', and thought, *but if you really do want to surprise them you should at least make sure you know where they might be and what might happen next as a result of your surprise.*

Ninja moves

What will happen next?

If you've exhausted all possibilities and decided your only course of action is to stamp your feet and go storming in, do at least make sure you go storming into the right place, have a valid reason and have understood the consequences of what might happen next. Play it out in your head to give you an idea of what's likely to happen next before you actually do it.

Even if you've got your facts right, this option rarely plays out well. This is a good example of when to pause and think about how to make a stealth-like Ninja move. One that will, overall, have the impact you want. Always seek opportunities that might be hiding in plain sight.

Tools and templates

Don't blow your own house down

We're all used to doing options appraisals and they mostly follow the Goldilocks and the Three Bears narrative.[34] But how often do you think through 'what will happen next' based on the options?[35] And how often do you think about the options for decision-making in terms of what will happen next?

ISWON™ is a great tool to work through before you make *any* decisions.

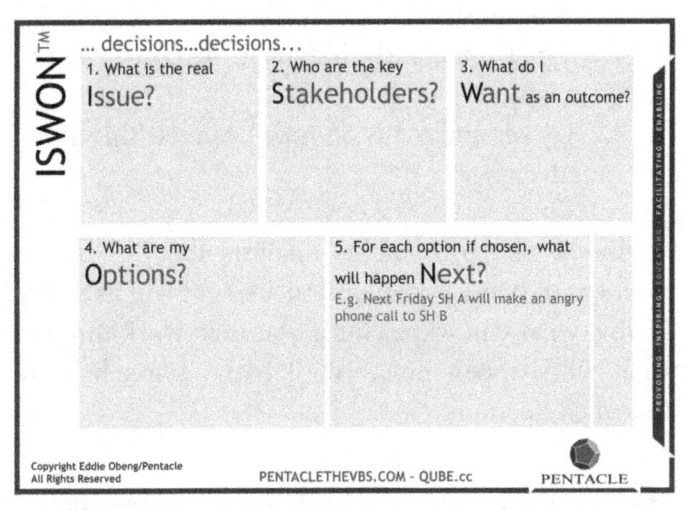

ISWON™
...decisions...decisions...

1. What is the real **Issue?**

2. Who are the key **Stakeholders?**

3. What do I **Want** as an outcome?

4. What are my **Options?**

5. For each option if chosen, what will happen **Next?**
E.g. Next Friday SH A will make an angry phone call to SH B

Copyright Eddie Obeng/Pentacle
All Rights Reserved
PENTACLETHEVBS.COM - QUBE.cc
PENTACLE

---

[34] One too hot, one too cold and one just right.

[35] The one that's just right might sound just right in terms of cost and outcomes. But has anyone really given any real thought to what's actually involved in delivering this option? If not, the following paragraphs on ISWON™ will give you more detail for an informed decision.

Take the previous challenge around the staff reward programme.

Issue: You're being asked to do something extra because someone else has failed to deliver, which isn't fair.

Stakeholders: The Boss, The Big Cheese, The Mini Cheddars

What I **Want** as an outcome: Support to do the things I think are important and not be the 'go to' to sort others' messes out.

What are my **Options**?

1. Stomp my feet, say no and do more interesting things instead
2. Agree reluctantly but make it clear I'm not happy
3. Say yes and focus on how I can use this to my advantage

Based on cost/benefits analysis for you in the moment of being asked, option 1 might win as you're getting what you want. But if you then work through what will happen next, you'll make a much more informed decision.

Stomp my feet, say no and do more interesting things instead

- More time to focus on doing things that will add value
- Boss not happy

- Boss stops supporting ideas
- Boss starts making you play the game more and you start to lose your freedom

Agree reluctantly but make it clear I'm not happy

- Feel frustrated and put upon
- Come to work complaining every day
- Lose motivation for the good stuff
- Go directly to page ??

Say yes and focus on how I can use this to my advantage

- Boss is delighted
- You can do this with your eyes shut but make a bigger deal of it outwardly
- Keep dropping into conversation all the things on hold just now so that you can deliver this project
- Assess how big an 'ask' you might get away with in the near future based on, sigh, all this hard work on top of your day job

Option 3 clearly is the right option.

It's sometimes hard to think this through on the spot. But if you have five minutes try it out on your next decision and you might end up making a much better choice. This is a classic, stealth-like, Ninja move.

Your reflection

You put the book down and reflect again on your decision to do the Boss's bidding on the last project. By stamping your feet and shouting that it's not fair, you'd have got out of the project but only suffered longer term. By saying yes and using it as an opportunity for trying some new things and building up some brownie points and kudos from other managers, you'll hopefully get more support for the next thing you want to do.

Challenge 4

Well, that does look innovative

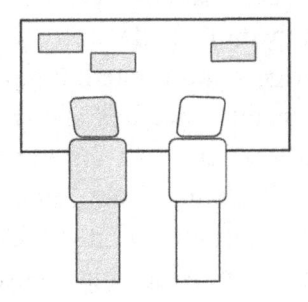

Eight months ago, you were selected to attend the inaugural organizational-wide leadership programme. It had potential. An eight-month programme with various events and speakers. At first you were quite excited. But the reality is it has been a typical sheep-dip approach with a focus more on management skills than leadership.[36]

Despite that, you're quite excited about the closing event, which Prof. Eddie Obeng will be running. You've read some of his work in various magazines and used his 'change types' approach from Sami's Fables quite a bit. You're therefore really looking forward to the

---

[36] You know, where getting as many as possible through the process with a generic learning package is more important than quality of content or assessment of people's learning needs.

insights he'll share at the closing event. And you need to be inspired. Nothing exciting has grabbed your attention recently.

The day arrives and the Prof doesn't fail to deliver. With his 'World After Midnight' video, his new world tools that he calls PETs (performance enhancement tools) and his general energy and enthusiasm for change, he's really motivated you.[37]

What really gets you excited, though, is the super reality virtual facility that he's showing you around on the projector screen. It's for doing all of those things everyone is talking about (digital office, virtual working, collaboration, productivity, innovation, culture change, removing hierarchy, empowering staff). This facility is called QUBE.[38]

First up it's a 3D space that has rooms (qubicles) that look like offices or workshop spaces. There are whiteboards, presentation screens, tables to sit at. There are avatars to represent everyone who's joined a qubicle. These avatars are autonomous and able to move around, as they might in real life. You can see some avatars are sitting at a table and some working on the whiteboard. He explains that they're in different

---

[37] 'World After Midnight': www.youtube.com/watch?v=w_GSToZBRxg
[38] Eddie likes to point out that it's not a platform or software as those things tend to focus mainly on technology. He describes QUBE as a facility with three legs. Technology (the virtual space), Education (the tools he uses called PETs) and Behaviours (the culture and way of working). This last bit, the human connections and behaviours, are, he says, why it works so well and what other digital solutions tend to lack. www.home.qube.cc

Challenge 4: Well, that does look innovative 69

sound zones so can be in the same room but having different conversations that they can jump in and out of. Like real life.

He then explains that visiting QUBE is like visiting a foreign country. One that has different rules you have to navigate and follow, a different language you need to learn to really immerse yourself. And that QUBE has been developed to change how we work. To make us more collaborative, productive and effective. To move us from hierarchy to alignment. To support creative problem-solving and innovation. To get us looking forward at what needs to be done rather than looking backward at what has been done.[39] It can move us from being office-based to being anywhere-based but that those who use QUBE even use it when they're in the same building as it's more effective than their face-to-face meetings.

'You have to try it,' he says, 'to really understand it. Like visiting a foreign country, you can read lots about it but you don't really understand how different it is until you visit. But if you really want to shift things, change your culture and behaviours, then you need a new language that everyone has to learn in a safe environment where everyone is equal.'

This, you think, looks like something that might help you deliver the goal you've set out for innovation:

---

[39] Here he mentions project meetings that tend to focus on reviewing the past month, that focus on targets being met and, if they haven't, why they haven't, before writing minutes about the meeting that focused on what happened in the past month and so on.

to change process, behaviours and create new ways of working. It also meets many of the wider programme aims such as digital working, empowerment and agility. Not only that but it was the Big Cheese who brought Eddie in to run this session so the Big Cheese must think this way of working is needed too.

You grab the Prof during the coffee break and talk about how you might introduce QUBE into the organization. He seems over the moon that someone is curious enough to ask about it. 'Let's talk next week,' he says, beaming at you, before turning to talk to someone else waiting to ask him a question.

You're really excited but think about how you might get this to work. Firstly, the Big Cheese is likely to be supportive of something as they clearly think the Prof has something to teach the organization.

Secondly, you have all those brownie points from the staff reward project so you could use that as leverage to try to get both approval and budget from the Boss to try it.

One week later…

You're ready for your call with the Prof. He calls and is full of energy and enthusiasm. You explain the challenges you face and how hard it might be to get traction, so he suggests a short proof of concept with a modest budget.

'We can make this work,' he assures you. 'I have many magic tricks up my sleeve.'

After the call, you're excited and set about preparing a short business case pitch, making sure to

Challenge 4: Well, that does look innovative 71

use all the latest buzzwords, linking it to the big change programme aims and the leadership programme. You then go to the Boss to pitch the idea. You mention the Big Cheese a lot, given it was the Big Cheese who brought in the Prof in the first place. And the fact that there's budget and you've yet to spend any of it.[40] And that you did run that last project successfully, you know, the staff reward project. After about 20 minutes or so the Boss reluctantly agrees but 'remains sceptical'.

Woohoo, you say internally as you leave the room. At last, something new and, dare you say, innovative.

The Prof suggested you gather a diverse group of staff to try out this concept with you. 'That way you'll get different insights and people talking about this in all different areas of the organization.' So, you start recruiting, using people in your pirate crew to help point you to possible candidates. You end up with a nurse, doctor, operational manager, lawyer, data manager, IT and a grumpy 'been there, done that, got the T-shirt' programme manager, all from different parts of the organization.

It's a few weeks later and you get started in your weird 3D office full of whiteboards, screens, chairs and even bean bags. You're all represented by square, brightly coloured avatars and have all joined from different physical locations.

---

[40] Even though you do have a budget you don't actually have permission to spend it. Empowered staff is very much some way off.

With some of Eddie's teaching and facilitation, this new team forms, collaborates and gets to work quickly. You focus on people, enablers for change, what processes need to change, what behaviours are needed and what areas need new ways of working. You all agree these are key for becoming an innovative organization. You do this not by talking and talking about what you could do but by working through a series of tools called PETs, which are in the expansive PET library.[41] You start with something called a 5Ps™, which is used to align the group around the task.[42]

Before you talk, Eddie asks you to place your ideas on sticky notes directly on to the 5Ps™ tool. Once you've done this, Eddie reads out what you've all written and checks in with everyone, one by one in alphabetical order, for any other comments. He calls this SpinCasting™ and explains that it means everyone gets a say and everyone knows when they'll be asked to comment based on their name. He also explains that by writing before talking you're much more likely to get everyone contributing equally and stop the conversation being steered by one opinion. Next you do a GapLeap™, which is essentially a 20-minute business case.[43]

---

[41] Performance Enhancement Tools.
[42] Remember the 5Ps™ stands for Purpose, Principles (things to do or not do), People (stakeholders), Process and Performance (what does success look like). It can be used as a project brief, communication or just to focus and align the team on the current activity.
[43] Template page 84.

Challenge 4: Well, that does look innovative

You're all amazed at how much you get done in one session by working in this way. Before the session is over, you capture and assign actions on the action board and have agreed that they can, and will, be done before the next session.

After just six weeks of meeting for an hour a week, you've created a framework for innovation for the organization. And now it's time to present the outcomes and your findings to the Exec team.

Current status ⊙ 97 ◐ 3

Decision time

Do you:

a) Write up the framework and prepare a presentation? (page 73)

or

b) Get creative? (page 75)

Write up the framework and prepare a presentation

As you sit down to start the tedious job of turning this into an 'acceptable' document you have a word with yourself.

This is going to take hours to do. And then there will be all the back-and-forth emails and dreaded tracked changes, which you'll need to apply to keep everyone happy before discovering the 14th version is pretty much *exactly* the same as the first version. But… collaboration and all that.

It will take at least six weeks, at which point everyone will have moved on and forgotten how great those six weeks on QUBE were. How easy and fun it was. And how bloody productive you were. The grumpy 'been there, done that, got the T-shirt' programme manager will have gone back to being grumpy and everyone will forget that for those six weeks he was quite chirpy.

So, no. You don't want to do it, but you think that this is the only way to ensure success at the next stage – by playing the game. Therefore, you open a blank Word document and save it as 'Innovation Framework V0.1'.

Current status ☉ 32 ◐ 2

After half an hour you pause.

Are you really going to spend hours and hours writing up a 40-page evidence-based document to support your 30-slide presentation about new ways of working and innovation? You know no one reads this stuff. It just sits in a drawer gathering dust. Surely, if you really want to make this change happen, then it really does need to start with you.

Current status ☉ 24 ◐ 1

If you want to continue writing the document, please turn to page 23.

If you decide that the change will start with you and that the rules of the game need to change somewhat then keep reading and get creative.

Get creative

'Let's do the whole presentation on QUBE,' you suggest to the team.

They rapidly agree and you set about creating a story to showcase all the work you've captured on the virtual whiteboards. Why write it all up when it's already there for everyone to see?

So, you're sitting with the Exec team in their big grey boardroom with QUBE projected on to the big screen, while the rest of the team are all in different physical locations but all in the same virtual room (qubicle). You quickly brief the Exec team on what's about to happen and then the avatars take over, presenting all the work you've done on the various whiteboards. They're zipping about the 3D room from board to board and having much more fun than you are in the stuffy Exec meeting room. They're massively enthusiastic about the process and sharing how much they've learned about virtual working, collaboration, innovation, agile delivery, productivity and creativity. 'And we did all this in just six weeks,' they keep saying.

'This,' they confidently suggest to the Exec team, 'is what we need to change how we do things, change the culture, behaviours and processes that will help us deliver the programme aims. It removes the fear, makes us all equal and aligned and gets us where we need to be quickly. It didn't matter what our job title was, we all had an equal voice. It didn't matter whether we were introverts or extroverts, we all had an equal voice. We properly listened to each other and aligned ourselves around a common goal. We were energized, motivated and really enjoyed working this way. This will enable us to do all the things you keep saying you want us to do.'

The Exec team look a little 'rabbit in headlights' but you think mostly in a good way. After some questions, which the team respond to with excellent answers, the Big Cheese says, 'Okay, we get it… but what do you need from us? Why are you here?'

You suggest a modest budget and their support would get you going, explaining that you'd like to try a few different things, such as training and project delivery, with a few different groups.

'Okay. Put a short one-page business case together and we'll get the funds signed off.'[44]

As you pack up your laptop and get up to go, the Big Cheese leans over and says, 'We had to say yes to one of your crazy ideas at some point.'

It's not quite what you wanted to hear but you're too excited and delighted with the outcome to care. Back at your desk you quickly log back on to QUBE to tell the waiting team the good news.

At last. Something innovative that could be utterly transformative. Your gut instinct to try a different approach has finally paid off. And your gut instinct to change the rules of how to present it really worked.

---

[44] This is the first time you've been asked to do a one-page business case. Just one page. Blimey. You still wonder why it's needed as the money seems to have been approved already but… you know… governance and all that.

Challenge 4: Well, that does look innovative

You can also use this as a case study to show how much time can be saved by not doing something the traditional way if it doesn't make sense. You feel like a Ninja.

Maybe, just maybe, you're in the right job after all. Full health resumed.

Current status ❤ 100 ⚡ 3

You're ready to leap forward. But first, that one-page business case.

You reflect back on the work you did with the team on QUBE in the last few weeks. One tool, called a GapLeap™, was described as a business case in 20 minutes.[45] You quickly log on to QUBE and flip to the whiteboard that's labelled GapLeap and there it is. You remember when you all filled this in.

1. The gap between where we are now and where we need to be:
   In this case: We don't have the tools, process or behaviours that enable us to be a flexible, agile and innovative organization.

2. If we don't fix it:
   Here you listed all the things that would continue to happen if the organization did nothing. Slow to respond to customers' needs, inefficient, slow to deliver patient outcomes, lose business, lose good staff and so on. You recall that after you'd written out the stickies you then organized them into a

---

[45] Page 84 for template and more details.

compelling story before reading them out and checking that everyone agreed with the story.

3. If we fix it:
   Here, all the positive outcomes and benefits of being… well… an innovative, flexible and agile organization.
   And finally,

4. Why not fixed:
   This bit was the clever bit. Because it wasn't about solutions it was about the problems that needed to be tackled to fix it. This created a list of things that could then be prioritized before coming up with ideas and solutions to fix them. The problem they'd prioritized was: 'We have fixed ways of working and fixed processes that stop us implementing change at scale.' They quickly realized that QUBE and the ways they'd pulled all this together could be a solution.

The Prof had then asked you to consider the 'Value at Stake' – the difference between how much it would cost the organization if nothing were done, such as lost revenue and staff turnover, and how much it would additionally save if it was fixed, such as more business, faster delivery of projects and so on (making sure not to double count). This was hard but they had a go and all agreed on rough figures that definitely made

Challenge 4: Well, that does look innovative

the 'Gap' worth fixing, even if it was only a high-level guess.

You quickly export the content from the GapLeap™ into a Word document as this will be more than enough for your one-page business case. You then just need to add how much you need to test the idea you all had that QUBE could be one of the solutions.

Blimey, you think. *That was quick. Could it all really become that easy that quickly?* But you're also cautious. Experience tells you that celebrating too soon always leads to pain. It's always two steps forward and one step back. You hope this time the Blockers are behind you, but you can't quite believe they are, and you suspect you'll need more stealth-like tactics to progress this, even with the Exec's backing. You'll need to find ways to 'sell' your idea as something that will benefit others. So, rather than ploughing straight on, you decide to see if Sami has any advice.

Sami's Fables Part 4

The reject

Sami was at a meeting about a very big organizational change programme. The room was full of Mini Cheddars and Blockers, clamouring to have their opinions voiced. The programme was being led by two of the elder Mini Cheddars, not because they had a track record in leading organizational change but because they were effectively redeployed and biding their time until retirement. They therefore had neither the skills nor skin in the game for an organizational change programme.[46] This only seemed to bother Sami.

Anyway, one of the 'exec' leads had been tasked with producing a framework for the programme. They presented it. There was lots of naysaying and loud objecting voices. After about 15 minutes they said, 'Alright, I hear you. I'll take your ideas and comments and come back with something different next week.' The 'exec' lead seemed very unphased at the objection to their work. Sami's interest was piqued.

---

[46] Just let that sink in for a while.

The following week the 'exec' lead got up to present again. First, they put the previous week's proposal up and then put a big red REJECT sign across it. 'You didn't like this one,' they said, 'so I took your ideas and views and came up with a new framework. Here it is.'

The new slide came up. There were lots of murmurs of approval and nodding of heads.

Sami looked at it again with wide eyes. It was *exactly* the same, except the colours were different and the boxes had been moved around. But the content was *exactly* the same.

When the 'exec' lead sat back down next to Sami, Sami whispered into their ear, 'It's exactly the same; you just changed the colours.'

'Shhhh,' they replied, with a deep chuckle. 'Don't tell anyone. It's a good trick and it always works but only while people don't know about it.'

Sami resolved to keep it a secret.

And use it wisely when needed.

But Sami is happy to share it with you. You need a few more Ninja moves up your sleeve if you're to get to the end of this adventure.

And, at the end of the day, if it gets people on board and behind you, even if they think it's their idea (not yours), then it's a very good move to have up your sleeve indeed.[47]

But shhhh... don't tell anyone.

Ninja moves

What do you think the answer is?

It can be really hard to get buy-in from others for new things or your own ideas. Our ancient brains are wired to see the new and unknown as a threat. If we can't see anything in it for us straightaway, we'll treat it with caution at best and dismiss it at worst. And anything that's less tangible – about culture, behaviours and changing what we know – is even harder because it suggests that what we've been doing up to this point is wrong.

When implementing change, you therefore need to be cautious, smart and use Ninja tactics. You need to introduce things in a way that doesn't scare people off or make them feel stupid if they

---

[47] You just need to get used to *never getting* the credit for your ideas. It's sometimes called invisible leadership, which is the best type of leadership for real Change Ninjas.

don't understand it, which will also scare them off. You need to invite criticism and comment on your ideas and take them into account before any formal pitch. Also use language that will sound familiar to those you're pitching to, rather than trying to be too smart with word salad.[48]

Ask yourself how often you've said something won't work before you know what it really is. Or dismissed the latest social media fad that the kids are all into. We all do it because it's easier to dismiss the unfamiliar than accept there might be a new or better way. And that's what your audience is likely to do when you tell them about your latest crazy idea.

Tools and templates

The 20-minute business case

In the last chapter you heard about the 20-minute business case called GapLeap™. But how is that even possible when typically, for a business case, you have to think about benefits, risks, options, costs, and get everyone to comment on it several times just to get the first draft? Sometimes a big chunky document with

---

[48] You know, when it's just buzzwords strung together to sound smart but has *zero* real meaning.

lots of detail is very much needed,[49] but sometimes business cases are done because that's what we always do if we want to change something.[50]

Use GapLeap™ with the team and you'll have a business case in 20 minutes maximum and it will be better than any other business case you've done before.[51] Because unlike most business cases where the solution is sort of already decided, GapLeap™ makes sure you know what the *real* problem is that you're trying to fix.

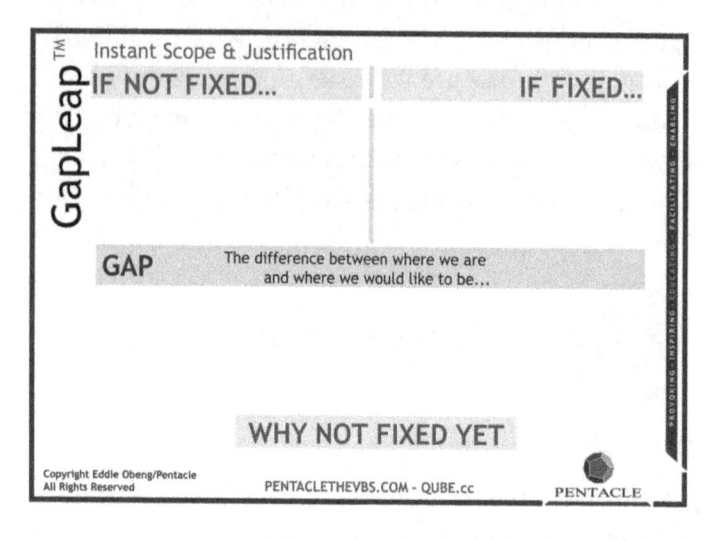

GapLeap™ — Instant Scope & Justification

IF NOT FIXED...	IF FIXED...

GAP — The difference between where we are and where we would like to be...

WHY NOT FIXED YET

Copyright Eddie Obeng/Pentacle. All Rights Reserved. PENTACLETHEVBS.COM - QUBE.cc

1. What is the 'Gap' that exists between now and where you want to be? This is the problem statement. Make sure it feels like a real problem statement and

---

[49] If you're, for example, going to be building a new hospital.
[50] That is mostly.
[51] Remember, this was used for the one-page business case to get QUBE moving.

not an assumed issue. For example, if someone says we need to be more efficient or we need to change the culture, push a little harder, asking why, until you get to the crux of the problem that feels right. Why do you need to be more efficient or change the culture? What's the actual 'Gap' we have?

2. If we don't fix it, what happens (and what's the cost of this)?

3. If we do fix it what happens (and what's the cost or savings of this)?

4. And, most importantly, *why* is it not fixed? *Not* what are the solutions.

5. Next create a value at stake for the problem, the cost to the organization of doing nothing (i.e. if all the 'if not fixed' things happen, how much does it cost us?) plus the additional cost benefits of fixing. This will give you an idea of how big the problem is. Don't worry too much about exactness but it will give you a useful comparison of the size of the problem against competing priorities.

6. Finally, put the 'why not fixed' in the order you think they should be done and estimate how much they might cost to fix.

This will give you the actual problem that needs fixing, risk, benefits, outcomes, areas to fix and estimated costs. If you do it as a team everyone will be aligned on the content, clear on how big the problem is and which areas need to be tackled first.

Not only is this good for business cases but it's also good to get people on board with your project. If they don't really understand why you're doing it get them to work through a GapLeap™ and they'll start to get insights into the problem and why it needs fixing.

Selling your ideas

Once you have everyone on board with the problem you'll then need to get them on board with your ideas. But you can also use them to make your idea *even* better using SlizedBread™. This will ensure that whatever your plans are, you've already thought of what everyone else's needs are, incorporated them and are much more likely to get a thumbs-up to a cracking solution.

Write down your idea:

Example: You sell chocolate and want to make more money. Your idea is to sell more chocolate by putting a new bar of it at the counter.

Now write down all the key stakeholders:

Example: Mum, kids, chocolate marketing department, shop manager, other customers in the queue.

Now imagine you're them. What do you (as them) think about your idea? What's wrong with it? Why won't it work in their eyes? And what's good about it (you may find there are things you hadn't thought of). Repeat for each stakeholder group:

Example: Mum (too much sugar); kids (too much choice, I can't decide what I want); marketing department (we'll need a new name, packaging and all the work that goes with it); shop manager (will I need more space? will I make any more money?); other customers in the queue (hurry up and choose).

Go back to your idea and change it based on this imaginary feedback. Incorporate the stakeholders' needs and expectations into your idea before you share it with them.

Example: I want to make more money by selling more chocolate, so I plan to introduce a box of tiny bars of existing chocolate. It will allow mum to reduce sugar intake, especially before dinner; the kids don't need to make choice at checkout but when they get home instead; marketing don't need 'new imaging/branding', they just need to shrink the wrapping; the queue isn't held up by kids making slow decisions and the shopkeeper makes even more money selling a box of chocolates rather than just a bar, and it might even appeal to the adults in the now fast-moving queue.

You just made your okay idea much better. And there's a good chance your stakeholders will buy into it.

Your reflection

You put the book down and realize how hard this might all be. Just simple changes have been a challenge, so trying to do something innovative that might shake up years of process and ways of working feels nigh on impossible. Especially given the number of Blockers you'll have to try to persuade. But it will be worth it, you think, because you've seen how things can be different, and in a very good way. This is the type of thing that excites and motivates you and is, after all, your overall objective. But Sami's Ninja moves will likely be required. In buckets.

Challenge 5

Virtually virtual

You're still celebrating your big win. Something you wanted to progress has got the go-ahead. Something that feels innovative at last and is ultimately about how staff can work in new and more collaborative ways. Finally, something that feels different, that may achieve some real tangible change and that the Exec team has agreed to sponsor (vocal support is key).

You're still amazed at how much work you've done in just six weeks using this virtual approach and using the embedded tools. And how quickly the diverse team came together and formed an aligned view on what was needed for the organization. And you're even more amazed that you have a budget signed off, which gives you enough to explore how you could use this new approach for different things to see where it works best.

You decide that a good place to start might be more general innovation training, which will not only help with creativity tools and thinking but also help others realize there are better ways to do the actual doing. Your great plan is to make new ways of working organic, viral if you like, and definitely *not* a top-down/sheep-dip/organization-wide roll-out approach.

You let IT know your plans and that at some point some others will be needed to install the app. And that's when your problems begin.

'We don't do manual installs so we'll need to package it. You'll need to wait until it gets to the top of the priority list. We'll give you a timescale in a couple of weeks, but it shouldn't take too long.'

It doesn't sound *too* bad… so you start designing the course and put feelers out for who might be a good first cohort. This is exciting. It feels innovative and transformative, if only on a small scale just now. This is the type of thing you signed up for.

A month later. No news from IT.

Two months. Your emails ignored, you wander round to the IT department.

'We'll let you know by the end of the week.'

Three months. No progress.

Four months. 'Could we manually install for just this small group? It's only 20 machines,' you ask. It seems like a very easy and obvious solution, especially as you know it will only take a couple of hours… tops.

'We don't have the resources,' they reply.

'Could you give me admin rights to do it? I'm happy to do it. It would only take a couple of hours… tops.'

'That's not how we do things. You don't work in IT, so no; you'll just have to wait.'

Challenge 5: Virtually virtual

By now you're beyond frustrated… the hours they've put into packaging something that may or may not be needed when all it needed was about two hours effort… max.

This. This is why the organization needs to change. How can it talk about digital workforce and innovation when it illogically follows due process for everything? Process that's so old that no one knows who even decided that it was the right process to follow in the first place. Process so convoluted that everyone assumes someone somewhere must know why it's like this and that this has been deemed the best way to do it.

You email, call, cajole, wander past their desks smiling, wander past their desks angry. You're a pain. You even beg. Nothing works.

It's now six months since you got the go-ahead. Six months to get a small application downloaded on to 20 machines. Six months in this supposedly agile, innovative and digital workplace.

Current status ⏱ 57 ◐ 2

Decision time

Do you:

a) Decide this is a battle not worth the effort? (page 92)

or

b) Fight the good fight? (page 93)

Decide this is a battle not worth the effort

You decide this isn't the battle to try to make a big stance over. No one ever wins against IT process, governance, security issues and convoluted decision trees. You know they're under-resourced for what they're asked to do, and you're running out of steam. You've tried and tried and got nowhere. You're one person and even your fellow pirates (who all have their own battles to fight) can't help you fight this behemoth of an organization.

It doesn't matter how much the messaging is about a digital workplace, being innovative, transforming and being agile in how we work, it's an organization stuck in old ways, governance and process. And people, lots of people who think it's legitimate to say 'that's not how we do things' (even if there's no logic in their decisions). No one is really doing anything about anything. No one really seems to want real change. It's all just lip service.

Current status ☻ 14 ☻ 1

Why should you keep putting yourself through this? It's energy-draining, exhausting, frustrating and totally unsatisfying. Maybe you need a new job.

If you're sure this is the right choice turn to page 23.

But if you've had a change of mind, reach deep into that rucksack, take a swig of keep-calm lozenge and a bite of a tenacity bar and prepare to fight the good fight. Keep reading.

Fight the good fight

Some battles are worth fighting for. And this is one of them. You know this is the big breakthrough you've been waiting for and that's worth pushing for. You know this will deliver what's needed. The very fact that this seemingly illogical barrier is being adhered to demonstrates the need to do something to try to change things.

But how best to go about it?

Firstly, you manage to get a 20-minute meeting booked in with the Digital Transformation Director to see whether they can help. In theory this should be right up their street.

But you know you need to approach with caution. Telling them directly that their team is being unhelpful and blocking you, even though you have a simple solution, is unlikely to get you anywhere. Ironically, you've since discovered that this particular director isn't too keen on other people's ideas in this space, given they're the 'expert' in this field. So you need to be really careful.

You wonder. *What would the Prof do?*

There's only one way to find out and you know exactly where he'll be. You quickly log on to the virtual portal and see that, yes, as you thought, Prof. Obeng is in his own virtual office. You send him a quick SOS message asking him whether he has ten minutes.

Current status ⏱ 68 ◐ 2

'What's up?' he asks.

You explain the issue to Eddie, who quickly asks, 'Tell me something that really bugs you about your other half?'

You're not sure what this has to do with anything but you go along with it.

'Mmmmm,' you say, 'he's really messy and leaves things lying all over. Sometimes there are about ten empty, mouldy mugs scattered through the house.'

'And have you asked him to stop doing that?'

'Of course. But it never works, however I ask, whether it's begging, anger or bribery. We just end up fighting about nothing.'

'That's because you're both coming at it from different perspectives with different reasons and different needs. Then add in some emotion and all logic flies out of the window. And has it ever occurred to you that maybe he knows something you don't and you just haven't figured out what that is yet?'

'About mouldy mugs?' you ask, anxiously glancing at your watch and thinking we don't have long here and I have a real problem to solve. You're really not sure where this is going.

'Maybe he's conducting an experiment in mould production in different parts of the house,' he suggests. You can hear him giggling and know it's a joke but also know that you're probably learning something. You're just not entirely sure what yet.

He brings up a tool called IDQB™ on to the virtual whiteboard and asks you to write on sticky notes what you really want to say about the IT issue.

Challenge 5: Virtually virtual

It feels really good to write it down as a rant and have someone see it.

He then asks you to think about what the real issue is. The 'I' in IDQB™.

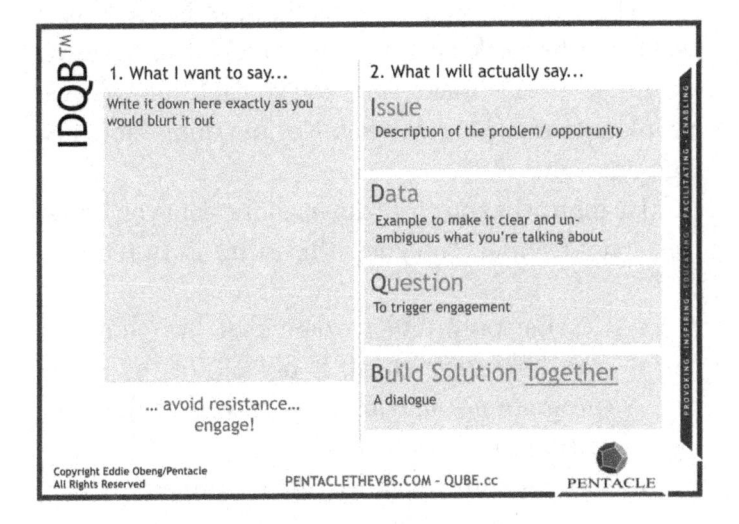

IDQB™	1. What I want to say...	2. What I will actually say...
	Write it down here exactly as you would blurt it out	**Issue** — Description of the problem/ opportunity
		Data — Example to make it clear and un-ambiguous what you're talking about
		Question — To trigger engagement
		Build Solution Together — A dialogue
	... avoid resistance... engage!	

Copyright Eddie Obeng/Pentacle — All Rights Reserved — PENTACLETHEVBS.COM - QUBE.cc — PENTACLE

You write a few things down.

- IT haven't delivered what they agreed.
- The programme you're running keeps getting delayed.
- The process is overly complex for the needs.

He keeps pushing you by asking 'so what?' and you keep going until you land on something that feels likes like the real issue:

'Six months ago, the Exec team all agreed to support testing of this new virtual approach as a potential way of delivering some of the aims of the transformation change programme and yet I've been unable to get access for the handful of people who've signed up to test it. This is now impacting on overall programme progress and outcomes.'

'That will do to get us going,' says Eddie, 'but I want you to work on this more before you have the meeting. Always make sure you've captured the real problem that needs resolving. Not the thing that's just bugging you.'

He then asks you write down all the data you know. Facts, not feelings. You guess this is the 'D' in IDQB™.

- It's the only tool to date that has shown it can help meet most, if not all, of the stated programme outcomes (as shown at the Exec meeting).
- IT leads are included in the project to help assess what changes to process and governance may be needed for scale-up.
- The security testing is complete, so I know it's safe.
- The course is set to run next week after rescheduling times.

… and so on.

'Now,' says Eddie, 'the "Q" of IDQB™. What's the question you'll ask the director?'

'How can we move this forward?' you suggest. Knowing, as you say it, that this won't be the right question.

'Make it something they need to commit to,' Eddie suggests, 'or something you can do for them.'

Finally, you settle on: 'Is there anything at all I can do to help, given the lack of resources within your team, to try to move things along so we can start the course as planned next week?'

'Good,' says Eddie. 'Now you can build the solution together, without the emotions you started this chat with. You have, or will have, a clearly stated real issue, with all the associated data, and a question that will lead to building a solution together. The question should always try to avoid a 'what will we do' approach as that can lead to it being too vague on who will do what. Let me know how you get on. Sorry, need to dash.' And with that his avatar disappears.

You keep working on the content before heading along to the meeting with the Digital Transformation Director later in the day. You have some notes scribbled but you've been through this a few times: state the issue, present the data (no emotion), ask the question.

Fifteen minutes later you leave the meeting with a smile on your face.

The result? 'It will be sorted by Friday – go ahead and let the course attendees know it's on.'

The clear facts made it really difficult for the director not to see how illogical the current process was. You also hope this will lead to some internal change to help with other things. It would also help the IT team massively. It can't be good to always be on the brunt end of angry customers.

You send Eddie a message on QUBE to let him know. It looks as if he's in a session with others, but he sends back a virtual high-five.

You try IDQB™ later at home… and a week later notice that, miraculously, there are no mouldy mugs lying around anymore.

Eight weeks later you're listening to a bunch of staff talking animatedly about the innovation training programme they've just attended in this weird virtual world and how they can't wait to start applying all the new tools and approaches they've learned on their projects. The buzz is so widespread that the communications team uses some virtual images from the training sessions in their poster campaign for digital working.

Current status ⏱ 88 ◐ 3

The virtual Eddie meets you later that week to congratulate you and remind you that change is hard but you're doing well. You're becoming a Ninja, he suggests.[52] Learning how to navigate people is the key element of change. It was a bit touch and go there for a while, you think, but you managed to get back on track. You needed to take a few sips of your reserve tonic but you got through and survived with all your lifelines in place. So, time for a nap to keep up your strength. But first, a bedtime story. You dig out your battered copy of Sami's Fables.

---

[52] This reference is starting to make more sense now. You even tell others about your 'stealth-like' approaches that are firmly under the radar.

Sami's Fables Part 5

Don't we have a plan for that?

Sami had been asked to attend a business continuity desktop planning exercise. Sami's boss said it was really, really important, nay essential, that Sami attend.

'We really must prepare for the unknown and be able to carry on delivering our services,' Sami's boss said. 'It's good governance and our team has to set examples around good governance.'

Sami looked around at the other people in the meeting. They all had their heads down. Grateful that they'd not been picked out for this particular activity.

Sami had decided to ask some clarifying questions, hoping that a mistake had been made and that Sami's boss would realize their error and ask someone else to attend because this was really not a Sami type of activity. It hadn't worked.

Finally, in a last-ditch attempt to get out of it, Sami asked, 'Could I make a suggestion?'

'Go ahead,' Sami's boss replied.

'Well, desktop exercises are all well and good but are unlikely to tell us anything we don't already know. Do you agree that what we really need are road-tested watertight plans that, should things go belly-up, we can implement immediately to mobilize staff?'

'Yeeesss,' was the nervous reply.

'So, to really develop and test these plans, why not develop the plans with a core team, close the office down for a week without telling anyone who isn't in on the business continuity testing and see what happens? It will identify what we haven't thought of, the real weak spots and fail points. We can plan it for a time that avoids things like month-end to minimize risk. We can even pre-warn our main stakeholders and explain that services might be a little slow for a couple of days.'

The team looked aghast. Had Sami finally lost the plot?

'Don't be ridiculous,' stuttered Sami's boss. 'We couldn't possibly think of doing anything so risky. What if we can't deliver our services? What will we tell everyone? What will managers think? Staff will just take the day off and do no work, and those that do work won't be able to access the file servers, and likely will say they can't access emails. It would be total chaos as no one would know what to do and nothing would get done.'

'Well...' continued Sami, 'isn't that the point? To test the business continuity plan, to see that it works and what everyone does come an actual emergency?'

'Ridiculous,' muttered Sami's boss again. 'Just make sure you attend the desktop exercise and report back at the next meeting.'

Later that day, Sami reluctantly accepted the meeting request for the event. Sami knew there was zero point asking whether they could dial in from home and resolved to volunteer to be one of the first to be 'taken out' in the first wave of what was sure to be a killer virus. Sami knew the whole focus would be about getting staff online and having access to email and mobile numbers to contact managers so they could communicate what was going on.[53]

The day of the event had arrived.

Sami knew that any bad behaviour would be reported back so had turned up on time and took a

---

[53] You might think, email? Really? ... But not everyone could access work email on their phone and not everyone had a laptop to use at home. This was very much pre-Covid times.

'keep-calm' lozenge before going. At a long stretch, it could be fun, Sami thought.

The room was full of weirdly excited people. As Sami sat down, Jim stood up at the front and asked for quiet, but everyone ignored him.

Of course Jim would be here, Sami thought, turning around and spotting Maya sitting next to the Steely Governance Manager, who was sitting behind three of the regular Blockers. *The usual suspects*, thought Sami, feeling that this was some kind of punishment. *Must not challenge the point of it. Don't ruin the school trip vibe that's going on*, Sami repeated over and over like a mantra.

Jim asked for quiet again and was still ignored.

'Everyone shhh,' said Maya loudly, lifting her finger to her lips.

Finally, everyone shushed.

'Unfortunately,' Jim started, 'today's business continuity exercise will have to be rescheduled because Bal, who, as you know, is Head of Business Continuity, is sadly not well and will be off work for a few days.'

There are a few groans of disappointment.

Sami started giggling uncontrollably and looked around the room. Geoff, who Sami had always thought was a bit dull and had never really spoken to, was proper belly-laughing, while others were giving him puzzled looks. Sami and Geoff shared a conspiratorial smirk.[54]

'You'd think they'd have a business continuity plan for the business continuity test planning not going ahead due to unforeseen circumstances, wouldn't you?' Geoff whispered to Sami as they left the room.

Ninja moves

Why Why Why?

Big organizations often lose sight of the real 'why' and just run through the motions of what they think they should do because that's how it's always been done or because one of the Mini Cheddars has been on a course or read a book. In the public sector, this is often about five years (at best) after the private sector has gone through the process and realized it was pointless, but they still do it anyway.

---

[54] Smirks aren't recommended. They're not clever. But sometimes a sneaky one will pop out before you realize.

Some things are necessary – like business continuity planning – but often focus on the wrong thing. In Sami's organization, the focus was always on staff accessing systems when not in the office. This seemed nigh on impossible to do, hence all the planning and what ifs and worry about emergencies and desktop exercises.

But then we had an emergency. A global one. And in just a couple of weeks MS Teams or Zoom was rolled out to everyone and everyone had a work laptop at home. This could have been done at any point pre-Covid to support the digital workplace, but it wasn't. So, the business continuity planning focused on a problem there was already a solution for that, for some reason, even though it had been procured, wasn't already deployed. It was therefore a pointless exercise. It focused on the wrong prob. Now if they'd switched off the internet for the day… that would have told them a lot of things they needed to know.

This is the same for many processes and systems. At some point they made sense but then the real 'why' is lost, yet everyone still follows the processes and protocols, even if they no longer make sense or achieve anything of value.

But… if you go in with your logic it will feel like a challenge to the other person. And when challenged, people will often fight back as the brain has switched off logic and switched on emotion, and emotion is screaming 'fight', or 'run for your life'.[55] You therefore need to act with stealth. Every time. Using tools such as IDQB™, where you share the issue and data and remove all emotion before asking the killer question, it ensures the logic bit of the other person's brain stays switched on, allowing you to build a solution together.

You should also seek out fellow humour conspirators like Geoff. They're hiding in plain sight and help ease the pain.

Tools and templates

Getting turkeys to vote for Christmas

Don't go in all guns blazing. Go in IDQBing. If someone is disagreeing with or opposing your change this is a great way to find out why and get them to change their minds. Complete the left-hand side. Write what you

---

[55] This is classic ancient brain technology. Your brain is continuously scanning for danger, and challenges feel like danger. This causes your brain to close down the processing plant (where logical decisions happen), because it's both energy-hungry and relatively slow, and instead switches on the fight, flight or freeze app.

really want to say. Don't hold back. It's cathartic. Just don't show it to anyone else if you value your job.

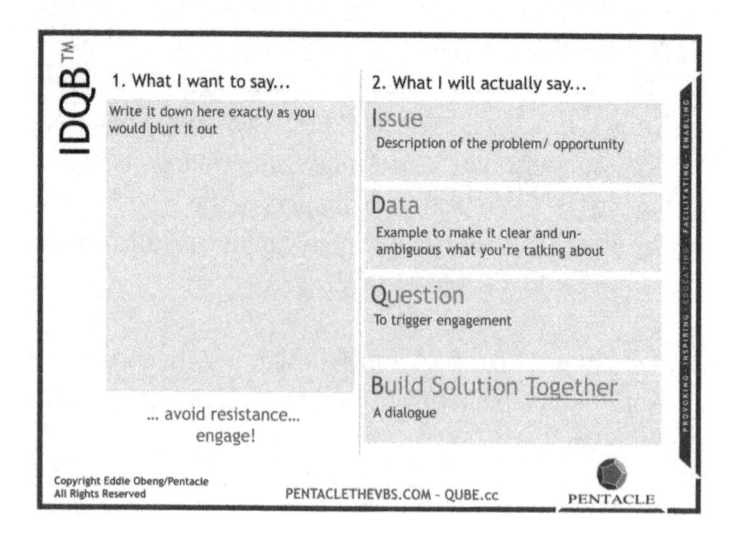

IDQB™

1. What I want to say...	2. What I will actually say...
Write it down here exactly as you would blurt it out	**Issue** — Description of the problem/ opportunity
	Data — Example to make it clear and unambiguous what you're talking about
	Question — To trigger engagement
... avoid resistance... engage!	**Build Solution Together** — A dialogue

Copyright Eddie Obeng/Pentacle All Rights Reserved — PENTACLETHEVBS.COM - QUBE.cc — PENTACLE

Then work through the right-hand side, identifying the real real issue (not the perceived issue).[56] This may take a while to get right. If you want a dog, for example, and the other half doesn't, the issue isn't that you want a dog. The issue is maybe that you often feel lonely and anxious when home alone. The dog is your preferred solution.

Then pull together the data – facts, figures, knowns (not feelings or opinions). Back to the dog issue. Data might be that your other half works away from home a lot. You're stuck in the house a lot. You need motivation

---

[56] Write the issue then ask yourself why this is an issue. Using why questions helps you dig deep.

to go for more walks, which will help with anxiety. You often feel anxious being home alone at night. You're new in this area and want to find a way to meet other people. You haven't yet… you'll notice… mentioned a dog.

Then, the killer question. Make it about something you can do, or they can do. Try to avoid asking, 'What will we do?' We is like the 'royal we' and tends to be a bit vague about who's going to do what. 'What are your objections to me having a dog as I think a dog would really help resolve this issue?' or 'What could you do differently to help me resolve this?'

Then build the solution together. For question one it would be hard for them to say no to a dog outright based on what you've presented. If they do have real objections, they'll present data too, in a non-emotional way, and you might find they have other solutions that could also work. The second question means they'll need to commit to action to help you and are more than likely to suggest you just get a dog. Either way you'll more than likely end up with a solution that works for you both.

It's quite hard to do and do well, so practise. Practise on the kids and significant others and you'll see some miraculous results. You might even end up with a dog.[57]

---

[57] This did in fact happen, after a training session. Six weeks later a dog was installed.

Your reflection

You put the book down. So much of Sami's story is familiar, you think, recalling similar 'processes' you've had to follow that make no sense or where there's a total lack of seeing the irony in decisions in the name of governance, or risk management or some such. And that last previous challenge with IT to get a small app installed was just infuriating when it had zero value and only caused more work for everybody. No one was winning in that situation. But using that tool IDQB™ was a win-win. You promise to practise it. A lot.

But you're well rested, well learned and it's time to get back to your journey. Remember, you have a bottle of humour pills in your rucksack if needed. And keep an eye out for fellow conspirators.

Challenge 6

Take two

Your journey is really getting going now. Some great things have been happening but it's still in small cohorts and mostly with people who already like change and are interested in trying new things.

Two things drop on to your radar this week. Both get you thinking.

Every year a cohort of nurses (often the same people) are invited to attend training to develop their leadership and change management skills. It's mostly in-house delivered, centrally held, spaced out through the year events and requires a lot of travel for the participants (they're based all over the country). In the last three years it's had minimal impact as a day spent learning about quality improvement is unlikely to turn them into quality improvement managers or experts when they get back to the firefighting day job.

You know that the staff attending these sessions get frustrated as it wastes their time for very little benefit. But they're keen to learn, which is why they keep turning up. In addition, the travel time (sometimes with an overnight stay) and having to fit in around childcare and other work priorities, knowing that no one will pick up on their work while they're away, means their energy is low before they've even started.

The second thing to catch your attention is leadership. Everywhere you look, people are talking about the problems we all have… 'If only we had the right type of leadership,' they say, like it's something you can buy from Amazon.

You do a quick Google search and the latest leadership trends seem to be exponential: collaborative leadership, collective leadership, inclusive leadership, liminal leadership, how to be a corporate rebel leadership. They all have great glossy looks and qualities that everybody would want but they also mostly look theoretical. Great to learn in a classroom setting but the reality of adapting those behaviours *and* then applying them in a work setting, particularly one with a very hierarchical structure that is still run like the original navy of command and control, is nigh on impossible. It just doesn't work. So, all you end up with is higher levels of frustration for those attending such courses, who often come back full of enthusiasm before being told 'that's not how we do things here'.

But back to the nurse leadership and change management skills programme. The sponsor has invited you to run something on innovation at one of their training sessions.

Current status 🕐 91 🌀 3

Decision time

Do you:

a) Accept politely and agree a date? (page 111)

or

b) Suggest something entirely different? (page 116)

Accept politely and agree a date

You accept and agree a date.

Current status ⏱ 69 ◐ 2

But...

This leads to a second decision. You could quickly pull together a traditional standard presentation, workbook, with a few small exercises thrown in before inviting them to 'get on with it' *or* you could use it as a test bed to try something you've recently been learning about what you think could be useful as an organizational-wide learning and insight session.

Decision time

a) Do something (yawn) traditional? (page 111)

or

b) Suggest something low risk but a bit different? (page 112)

Do something (yawn) traditional

Are you really just going to say yes and do the easy option, knowing it will have zero impact? It might only take you a couple of hours to prepare the session, but you know full well that a day telling people what innovation is and how they might do it will do nothing other than waste their time. Worse, they're likely to become even more frustrated as they know they've just been shown something that they need and want but realize they have no real hope of getting. A bit like orphans at a sweet shop peering through the window.

Current status ⊙ 37 ◐ 1

Check your health levels. You took a big hit there. No one wins from this approach – you, them or the organization. More decisions.

Should you:

a) Just take a short cut to the end? (page 23)
b) Suggest something low risk but a bit different? (page 112)

or

c) Suggest something entirely different? (page 116)

Suggest something low risk but a bit different

Okay, so you've still taken a relatively easy low-risk option but you'll use it as a test case for something new to the organization. Your plan is not to tell them what innovation is but to take them through a process that will give them their own insights into what they could actually start to do that would help them do their job better. Something that will give them new tools and the confidence to start challenging the status quo a little more, which longer term should help change how they all work.

And this magical tool? You recently signed up for the IDEO Acumen Human-Centred Design course, which not only was free but was very very good.[58,59] Everything about it – the set-up, the challenge, the teaching, the peer review and the process. How did you not know about this before?

Yes, user design has been a thing for ages and grows every year across organizations as a great approach to use. But what you've experienced to date has just felt like the same old thing with the new buzzword of user design being added as an afterthought.[60] This course was a great eye-opener. And it was practical. You know you're late to the game but when you talk about it you realize everyone thinks they're already doing it because they're going out with their ideas, their websites, their data reports and asking for feedback. And because they're getting feedback from users they feel they've developed user-designed solutions. No one you talk to explains how they agreed what the problem was in the first place that needed their solution or how they checked that it was a real problem for the user in the first place. Asking for feedback on your website that

---

[58] https://acumenacademy.org/course/design-kit-human-centered-design/
[59] If you haven't done this yet in real life you really should.
[60] Similar to innovation, digital, collaboration, etc.: new words, same old process.

you think solves a problem may improve your website but it doesn't mean anyone is going to use it. Especially if it's responding to the wrong problem or isn't the solution the users want for their particular problem.

You decide to run a session on user design using the Design Thinking Bootleg Crash Course you recently discovered from dSchool Stanford.[61] It's a fun and creative way to learn about user design but more importantly leads to personal insights that can be applied to work. And personal insights are by far one of the best ways to learn. You decide to follow this activity with some creative problem-solving tools that are easy to apply to any level of problem using questions such as:[62]

- 'What's your 'Wouldn't it Be Nice If… (WBNI)' statement for this particular challenge area?[63] (This helps with knowing what success or the end goal looks like.)

- 'Why do I need to solve this problem?'[64] (This checks that by solving this particular problem you'll get the outcome you need.)

- 'Why haven't I already solved this problem?'[65]

---

[61] https://dschool.stanford.edu/resources/design-thinking-bootleg. Another free resource.

[62] Example: The kids are bored and distracting me from my work.

[63] Example: WIBNI everyone was happy and relaxed.

[64] Example: Because I can't get my work done, which makes me anxious.

[65] Example: Because I have too much to do to give them my attention.

… before turning the answers that resonate into further questions by adding 'How might we?' at the start.[66] These questions then help with idea generation.

The training day arrives and it's gloriously sunny. The room, however, is dark and dismal. So you suggest you all decamp to the grassy area outside. They're shocked, but quickly agree and pick up their chairs and head out to find a nice spot to sit in. Instantly, the mood is lifted and there's eager anticipation.

What follows is a day full of fun, creativity and laughter. The morning crash course process involves building prototypes from boxes and craft material. They rarely, if ever, get to do fun things at work, so moods are elevated and energy is high.

The afternoon creative problem-solving session creates lots of 'aha' moments and ideas for real problems start to flow once you throw in some real challenge questions. Ideas that go beyond the normal answers. Ideas that are new and innovative. Everyone leaves with smiles on their faces and still full of energy.[67]

Most importantly, they have both insights and practical tools they can start to use straightaway and know that the tools will work. They don't have life-changing statements about 'vision' and 'values' but things they can do easily, questions they can slip into everyday meetings

---

[66] How might we organize my work schedule better? How might we combine work and entertaining the kids? How might we reduce the list of things I need to do?

[67] Unlike typical sessions where everyone leaves with low energy and worrying about getting back in time to pick the kids up or missing the train that will get them home *before* ridiculous o'clock.

that will start to shift thinking around problems and solutions that should give them a bit more freedom to both challenge and do things differently.

They may not end up innovating at scale, but you're pretty certain that with their direct teams they'll feel confident they can resolve some of the issues and do so from their end users' perspectives.

You also feel quite energized. The session design worked and can be reused, could easily be taught as a train the trainer exercise and therefore will be relatively easy to scale up.[68]

Current status ☻ 69 ☻ 3

That was a good choice. But there's also another good choice. One where you 'Suggest something entirely different'. If you want to see what that one does keep reading.

If your curiosity is not piqued, go straight to the next chapter.

Suggest something entirely different

'What's your overall budget for the training for the year?' you ask the programme sponsor. They tell you and it's an okay amount. Not a lot but enough to cover the usual booking of venues, catering, travel, materials and one or two external speakers. You have an idea, but you don't want to spring it on them and potentially scare them off.

---

[68] Take care though. News might get out and you may be inundated with requests, and you do get bored rerunning the same things. Train some others up quickly in delivering this.

Challenge 6: Take two 117

You wonder whether the IDQB™ tool is the right one to use but there isn't an issue at stake here.[69] You just need a way to get your idea across without scaring them.

You grab one of those mobile flipcharts and suggest you get a coffee in the only comfy area in an office for 2,000 staff.[70] Once you're settled you get the flipchart out and start working through a 5Ps™ exercise.[71]

'I'd like to understand more about the programme,' you say. 'Is it okay if I ask you some questions?'

'Sure,' replies the sponsor.

'Okay. First up, what's the **P**urpose of the training?'

You then structure the rest of the conversation, working through the other **P**s, filling in information for **P**rinciples, **P**eople (stakeholders) and **P**erformance. The fourth **P** is for process, but you say you'll come back to this.

You then read through what you've captured to check it makes sense. The sponsor is pretty impressed by how quickly you did this and more crucially that what they want as an outcome (performance) isn't necessarily what the current process results in.[72]

---

[69] Page 106.

[70] This is 16 bucket seats next to the vending machines. Tables invariably covered in salt from the lunchtime crowd who couldn't get a seat in the canteen. Because they're not in the canteen, only next to it, the canteen staff don't clean these tables after the lunchtime period because that's not their job.

[71] Remember you used this to align the pirates on page 50.

[72] In this case, to increase confidence, provide tools that can be used in the work setting; build a network of nurses to lead change across regions.

After some more discussion you say, 'Now I understand it more would it be okay if I make a suggestion?'[73]

You know that given the travel issues running this virtually would be a great idea. Especially if it introduces the concept of virtual learning and new ways of working. But it's still early days for digital working and you don't want to scare them off with your 'madcap' idea.[74] Or get them into a place where they say well it's a great idea 'but it will never work' or 'they'll never go for it.'[75] You need to word this very carefully.

'So, you've been running these events face to face for three years, six sessions a year to build skills, and it's worked to some extent, but you want to try and get more from it in terms of outcomes, is that right?'

'Yes,' they reply.

'The idea I have is quite similar to what you've been doing in that we design a similar number of sessions that teach them something new that can be used immediately in the workplace. But instead of doing it face to face over the year, we squish up the equivalent of the six days over a two-month period. We'll have short teaching workshops once a fortnight and small project team sessions

---

[73] If you ask for permission before sharing ideas rather than blurting out 'I've got an idea', you're much more likely to get a warmer reception.

[74] Remember this is pre-Covid, and MS teams and other digital working tools were still on a list of IT priorities to be done, at some point!

[75] Something you hear often from managers as a vague attempt to disguise their fear of the unknown and worry that it will mean more work for them.

in between where we get them to work on a real work challenge using the tools we've taught them.[76]

'And we'll do it all virtually so we don't need to worry about travel or their work piling up as the sessions will be short enough to fit in with the day job. We can even give them a virtual coffee space for getting together informally for action learning sets.

'I know it will work because we've tested this approach already with the innovation cohort and the outcomes we achieved were pretty much the outcomes you've described. The added bonus of no travel, one of their biggest complaints, disappears, and you can give them their own safe space to get together and create that network you want for learning and peer support.'[77]

As you're saying this you're writing down some of the key actions such as 'design workshops', 'identify challenges for small project teams', 'set up user access to the digital platform' in the Process bit of the 5Ps™ on your flipchart.

'I'm in,' they say after a bit more discussion. 'When can we start?'

Current status ☙ 72 ☯ 3

---

[76] This is a good way to teach. It makes it real. A bit like at school. If your teacher just tried to teach you angles or fractions, it was really hard for many. If they talked about a pizza and you were all going to get a slice and asked you to work out the fractions and angles, it wasn't only a whole lot easier but also made sense as something useful to learn.

[77] Okay, you just didn't come up with this off the top of your head. It's one of the Prof's tools called 'Future Familiar'. Describe your idea as similar to something they already know, which removes the shock, before then adding why it's different and how you know it will work.

What happens next is that you design a leadership and change programme for a nine-week period. You set up four two-hour workshops knitting together a toolkit that the nurses can use immediately in the workplace. You set up weekly peer sessions to consolidate learning from the workshop and for members to support each other.

You select three real projects that they'll work on in small groups during the programme, which will help embed the new tools/processes/learning while also delivering real project outcomes. It all costs less than the available budget and is carbon neutral, which will please the carbon neutral stats guy.

A few weeks later the course starts. You can hear that everyone is a bit nervous of getting together virtually. They're a bit shy and all have their headsets on mute. But, after a quick warm-up to get to know each other, the participants have changed their avatar T-shirts to something personal, met and formed their small project teams and even come up with team names. They're having a blast. You can hear how relaxed and excited they are even though they were all quite nervous at the start. They've also set up their weekly coaching sessions and are ready to learn.

By the end of the nine-week programme you've created an amazing cohort of nurses who are now connected and keen to help each other do their jobs better, to look at national requirements for patient safety that also meets the needs of their local stakeholders.

Not only that but this slightly nervous cohort have presented their work and learning experiences in a virtual 'show and tell' session to senior managers and directors. When asked for a comment from their director, their response is more than you'd expected.

'I'm blown away with the level of confidence in the room that wasn't there before this programme,' the director replies.

There's an overwhelming 'we don't want this to stop' from the cohort, so you suggest they meet regularly using this digital approach for virtual coffee and keep working, learning and collaborating in this new normal. Next, they make a video of their experience before presenting what happened at conferences over the following year, all of which they do without feeling that they have to ask for 'permission'.[78]

Three of the cohort ask whether they can become mentors on the next programme. This, they say, is how they want to start working and collaborating at scale. You are, it would be an understatement to say, quite delighted.

With a small budget, some creative thinking and the bravery of others to try something completely different, you've transformed what was a tick box training programme into a new way of learning and working. This has also given you a great case study of how you've helped create those leaders everyone says

---

[78] QUBE – From Here to There https://youtu.be/sgxhoHlntPo

the organization needs to deliver the changes they want. Surely it will be plain sailing from here on in?

Current status ☻ 97 ◑ 3

You're almost back to full health. Things are going well. That last story had two great outcomes both using very different solutions. Both looked at the core problem and came up with creative solutions to meet user needs. And both required you to think carefully about the approaches you took to get buy-in from the sponsor and users. But there's always more to learn, so you wonder what other Ninja moves Sami might have on approaching things in novel ways.

Sami's Fables Part 6

The wasp, the volcano and the sting

Sami attended a lot of events with a lot of senior people to talk about the organization, its needs and ideas to meet these needs. Leadership came up every single time.

'We need some strong leadership in this area,' the managers would often say. Sami always wondered where they thought this 'leadership' was likely to come from given they were, at least on paper, the very people they thought they needed.

Sami had to refrain from saying this out loud. Sometimes Sami would quietly mutter, 'I don't see anyone else's cars in the car park.' But Sami knew that other than with Geoff and a few other pirates, saying this out loud was at best pointless, at worst something Sami would get into trouble for. Sami knew this because once Sami had said it a bit louder than normal and Maya overheard and pulled Sami aside before pointedly pointing a finger at Sami and explaining this was bad behaviour before then telling Sami's boss, who then also told Sami how bad this behaviour was.

Another thing that came up a lot at these events was the word 'collaboration'. So much so that Sami had added it to the buzzword bingo board that came in useful for dull and pointless meetings.[79]

'We need to collaborate,' a Mini Cheddar would bellow before following up with, 'but we should lead the collaboration because we know what the right solutions are.'[80]

So, when Sami and a couple of other pirates had been requested to put together a 75-minute session on collaboration for 200 senior managers in groups of 30–40 as part of a regular senior management meet-up, Sami had thought this could be a real opportunity for managers to finally get real insight into what collaboration actually was.

Typically, these sessions were run as follows:

1. Put people into groups of eight or ten at tables.

2. Describe an obvious but vague challenge question. Something like 'we need more leadership'.

---

[79] That is, most of them.
[80] Sigh…

3. Provide each group with a flipchart and ask them to nominate a scribe.

4. Get the group to capture obvious ideas to the obvious question and obvious reasons why the obvious ideas wouldn't work (like we don't have the right leadership) before asking the scribe to feed back to the wider group a summary of the discussion.

5. Scribes then read, in turn, verbatim from what's captured until everyone falls asleep.

6. A tea break follows before heading to the next room to repeat with a different but still obvious and vague question.

7. Repeat until the end of the day, with lunch at some point. Free lunch. Ideally a free buffet lunch. Ideally a free hot buffet lunch.[81]

---

[81] Observing the buffet lunch never failed to amuse Sami. Especially a hot buffet. The type that has a choice of, say, lasagne, veg curry, chicken in a cream sauce with accompanying potatoes, rice, veg and a salad bar. The type where everyone eagerly lines up (reminiscent of school days?) before dutifully putting a bit of everything on their plates. What generally followed was quizzical looks at Sami's choice of just one of the meal options and asking 'is that all you're having?' Sami wondered, quietly of course, and not out loud, whether when they visited restaurants they would ignore the menu and instead say, 'Waiter, bring me a bit of everything you have on one plate.'

In short, they achieved very little, but everyone assumed that all their wise (obvious) words captured on sticky notes would henceforth be delivered. By someone. Not them. But someone. Because they were such good thoughts so why wouldn't they be taken forward by the leaders in the organization.[82]

But Sami and the pirates thought they could do something different, and try to get some real value from the session. Some real insights and real learning about how to collaborate. They started to bash out some ideas, but nothing landed. And then Sami recalled the business continuity exercise that didn't happen because only one person had access to the business continuity plan testing plan, and they were off sick so the testing of the business continuity plan couldn't go ahead.

'Everyone was really up for that desktop exercise,' Sami explained, 'and they were really disappointed when it didn't go ahead. Could we do something similar? Create a scenario and get them to play it out? One that requires them to properly collaborate? First-hand experience will lead to lots of insight and learning. A desktop collaboration exercise!'

The team thought this was a cracking idea and set about making it happen.

---

[82] Oh wait…

The wasp

First the team had created an emergency scenario. They decided on something that couldn't ever really happen to allow an element of fun, but something that would need the same services as a real scenario. The scenario they picked was giant killer wasps emerging from an erupting volcano.

They then turned this story into a black-and-white emergency news broadcast describing the situation and decorated the room with some 1950s killer wasp film posters to help set the scene.

The 40 managers in each session were then assigned to different teams, each representing an organization that, in a real-life work emergency scenario, would likely be involved, such as government, local authorities and health boards.

The volcano

Before the session started one of Sami's colleagues explained the rules and aim of the exercise. There was a *lot* of emphasis on it being 'a collaboration exercise' and the aim was to work together and respond collaboratively to an emergency that was about to unfold. The video was then played, and the game launched.

Once the exercise had started, teams were invited to collect more information every ten minutes. They were able to choose between scientific data, tweets or newspaper headlines. Additionally, general updates were provided throughout the game.

During the planning and testing of the exercise Sami and the other team members had felt it was creative and fun but also had clear purpose. They thought that, finally, insights would emerge, collectively, about what real collaboration was. They expected participants would discover that collaboration wasn't about inviting others to work with you on shared problems and adopting your solutions, but that collaboration was about working out loud together on the real problem and coming up with solutions together that would have the biggest impact.

The team also hoped that, finally, these senior managers would see that they were the leaders, that it was only their cars parked in the car park, and that no one else was coming to save them. The team were also assured that this would work when the Big Cheese let them know they would be popping into each session (they had to run it six times over two days) to observe the outcomes.

What, Sami and the team thought, could go wrong?

The sting

This. This is what happened. At every one of the six sessions.

1. Sami and the team don't notice but they'd just freaked everyone out and the entire room was in panic mode.[83]

2. When the bell rang for them to collect information updates, pretty much everyone chose to collect tweets rather than science updates. This made no sense, so the only conclusion that could be drawn from this was that there had recently been a lot of discussion about the organization using social media more.

3. The tweet updates were intentionally funny. The teams didn't find them funny but did find them frustrating.[84]

4. This didn't stop them collecting further tweets at the next information drop.

---

[83] It seemed they really liked the regular flipchart exercise, and no one had prewarned them this was going to be different. They've internally reacted as if a sabre-toothed tiger had jumped out at them. This wasn't familiar and their brains sensed danger.

[84] Example tweet from @BigRab_73: 'There's a great big stingy thing ootside ma windae.'

5. The emphasis was again made about collaborating, but nobody shared the information they collected with anyone else. Especially the team who went for actual scientific data. They smugly guarded their information closely. To themselves. Discussing in hushed tones that they could 'win this game' if they kept it quiet.

6. A general update was provided at half-time. The update stated that there was now a vaccine available to protect against the wasp stings. The (real) scientists in the room started arguing with Sami and the team that the data being provided was factually incorrect. A vaccine could not be developed in such a short time they claimed, but after some discussion they accepted that an existing antidote could have been sourced and carried on with the exercise. Confusingly (but thankfully) they seemed willing to accept the story itself of giant killer wasps escaping from an exploding volcano just 30 miles away.

7. After 40 minutes everyone seemed to be getting quite quite angry. They were sitting at their tables waiting for something to happen and someone telling them what they needed to do. None of them thought they should be actively doing anything because that was always someone else's job. 'In real life,' one Mini Cheddar said, someone else would make the big decisions about what

needed to happen. 'The leaders would tell us what to do,' they cried.

8. Some individuals did try to go to the other teams to suggest they all pool the information and ideas they had together, but they were mostly ignored or shouted at, so gave up. When they returned to their own teams they were ignored even more as they found that everyone was shouting at everyone else and no one had noticed them leaving or returning.

9. As the teams started to realize that some teams had important data they weren't sharing, fights started to break out. Thankfully they were verbal but, still, they were full of real rage.

This is what happened – at every single one of the sessions.

The Big Cheese was wide-eyed and speechless.[85]

So not much collaboration happened. Well, no collaboration happened. But it did provide a lot of insight. Just not the anticipated and hoped-for insight.

And, of course, the feedback after was terrible. Everybody thought they'd been set up. They hated it. They learned nothing. They felt tricked. Which of course had not been the intent at all. It was meant to be a

---

[85] This was a first. The speechless bit.

fun way of understanding what collaboration really meant. And to show them they could step up as the leaders that they were purportedly to be.

Ninja moves

> **Taking the sting out of it**
>
> Don't try to be a smartarse.[86]
>
> Not everyone is likely to feel the same way about your ideas.[87]
>
> In fact, to many, your ideas are really ugly babies.[88]

---

[86] Sami does accept that there was a little bit of smartarsery going on here. A little bit of we'll show them where they're going wrong.

[87] Which is probably also good advice the author of this book should take on board in relation to this book.

[88] You know, when people at work have babies and they bring them in to show off and everyone says 'ohh your baby is so cute'. Well for many people babies aren't particularly pretty or cute, in fact they can look quite ugly. But of course you don't say that. You go out of your way to say the opposite but whisper to your colleague later, 'That was some ugly baby.' All that matters is that mum thinks they're the most beautiful baby in the world. Well, ideas can be a bit like ugly babies. But in this case it really matters what everyone really thinks of it and not just mum.

If you do go ahead with an idea and it's a spectacular failure, especially one that involves a lot of people, learn from it (smart failure). Embrace it as an opportunity for discovery. Interview people to gain insights into what went wrong. Show your humility. Tell them your intent was good and that you accept the execution could have been better.[89]

Before you launch a new thing... drink your own champagne. If you tell others about user design, customer insights, making sure you've identified the right problem to solve, then make sure you use the tools yourself. Don't get carried away with what you think is a good idea without putting in the work needed to check it's a good idea and meeting a real need, as there's a good chance it's really an ugly baby.

Try using a user-centred approach. If you have time, human-centred design works very well. If you're in a rush use Aladin-Journey™, which walks you through the user journey.

Finally, it's okay to introduce fun. Just not at others' expense.

---

[89] Top tip. Use 'and' not 'but'. For everything. It stops you saying, 'I like this but...' (thereby negating the like bit). Saying 'I like this and...' turns it into an opportunity for improvement.

Tools and templates

Human-centred design follows five key steps:

First imagine you're a bank and want to create services that actually satisfy customers.

Empathize – understand the user issues by interviewing them to see what their personal challenge is. This is a divergent exercise to collect as much information as possible.[90] You can bring this information together to create a WIBNI statement. Wouldn't it be nice if...

> Example: Wouldn't it be nice if... Customers could talk to someone human when they have bank password issues to allow them to fix it without getting passed from department to department, each asking for their forgotten password.

Define – create a problem statement (converge all the data you have) that if resolved would meet the users' needs and deliver the WIBNI statement. Check that the problem statement, if resolved, would fix the user issues and deliver the outcomes required.

---

[90] Another useful framework is the Design Council Double Diamond approach, which goes through a series of divergent and convergent steps. www.designcouncil.org.uk

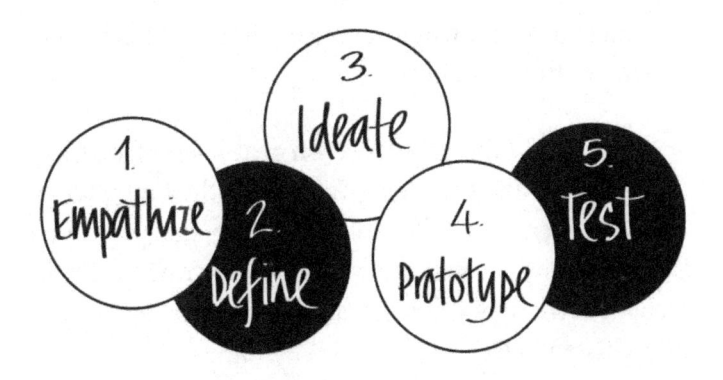

Example: The problem is that our customers get frustrated with password reset services when they're locked out of their accounts as it's frustrating and doesn't fix their needs easily.

Ideate – develop ideas (diverge activity again). As many as possible. Use the phrase How might we…? to help create ideas. If you come up with an idea that's still vague, turn that into a question using How might we…?

Example: Idea – create a 'locked out of bank account' hotline.

How might we create a locked out of bank account hotline?

Prototype – build a prototype of the best idea. It should be rough and ready.

Example: You can mock up a website in PowerPoint pretty quickly. Or create a quick flowchart of questions that would get users to a real person on the hotline quickly.

Test – test the prototype on real users. Don't ask them if they like the idea. Watch how they interact or behave when you take them through the prototype process. How are they interacting with your mock-up website? Are they still frustrated or do they feel they're being listened to?

Example: Working through a process of questions with a real user will quickly identify the flaws in the process before you've even thought of developing the code.

Then, and only then, should you start to develop the solution.[91]

But if you don't have time to do all of this you could instead use:

The customer journey genie lamp

Just like rubbing Aladin's lamp makes the genie appear, completing Aladin-Journey™ on your end product will make you appear like a genie(us).

---

[91] This, although quite ancient, describes the process in action. 'ABC Nightline – IDEO Shopping Cart' – www.youtube.com/watch?v=M66ZU2PCIcM

Aladin-Journey™

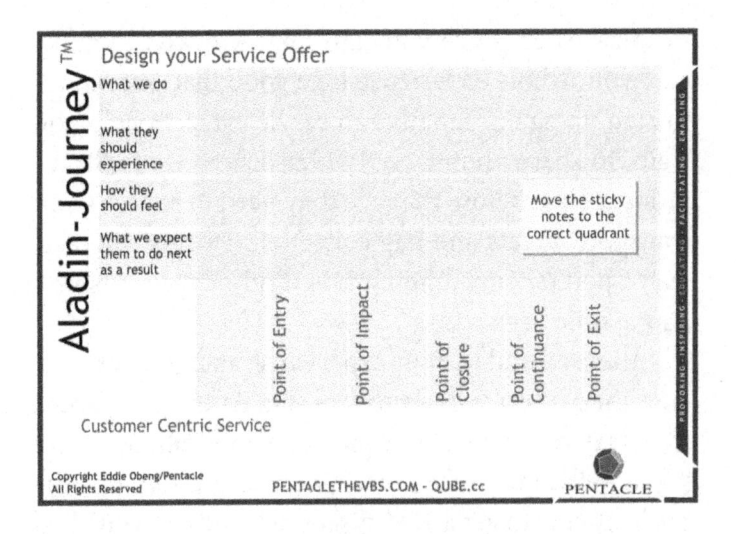

Design your Service Offer

- What we do
- What they should experience
- How they should feel
- What we expect them to do next as a result

Move the sticky notes to the correct quadrant

- Point of Entry
- Point of Impact
- Point of Closure
- Point of Continuance
- Point of Exit

Customer Centric Service

Copyright Eddie Obeng/Pentacle
All Rights Reserved
PENTACLETHEVBS.COM - QUBE.cc
PENTACLE

This tool gets you to think about each step in the customer journey. For example, if you're building an online learning programme you shouldn't just focus on the content and hope the learner signs up and pays attention. You need to design the programme to ensure the learner signs up, learns something, goes on to apply that learning, comes back for more and tells their friends about it. Thinking through what you expect the student to feel, experience and do after they've signed up will lead to a much better programme that delivers real outcomes.

Think about those companies that organize running events. First, they tap into their target (biggest) market with relevant marketing. For running this is often a younger crowd. 'Run your personal best at the UK's flattest 10k and be in with a chance of winning a trip to Ibiza'. Then, once you sign up, they need to make sure your whole experience is so good that you'll want to sign up again. Emails before the event to help you train, to share photos on Twitter or join up to Strava groups. Then before the race they need to ensure good transport, toilets and bag collection. During the race, water points, encouraging DJs. End of race, T-shirts and goodie bags.

These all add to your experience, and good experience means you're likely to repeat it. After the race, did they text you your chip time, take good photos, send you a well done you're amazing email and sign up now for next year to get a 10% discount? And did you? Did you sign up?

Thinking not just about the product (the race) but the entire experience and behaviours of customers will mean you're much more likely to build a successful product. And that's because you'll have also thought about what you want them to do next and built that into the product design. Things that will make them do what you want them to do next. It's a way of doing user design without having any real people to do user design on. Walk yourself through each step of the journey and you'll end up building in things that will ensure they feel what you need them to feel, and they'll do what you need them to do.

Your reflection

Well, you think, still laughing at the @BigRab_73 tweet, you did okay on that last challenge. Not only did you manage to sell two novel ideas but you also introduced all these great user design tools that would avoid others making the same mistakes as Sami. You're learning fast. Go Change Ninja!

Challenge 7

Shall we just do what we always do and expect different results?

You open up your inbox… the one at the top of the list just has the word 'Help' as the subject heading. It's from someone you don't know. You're intrigued. You decide your year-end review paperwork can wait because, while it's apparently imperative that you complete and submit the paperwork for your year-end review, the Boss has yet to set up time for your actual year-end review.[92] It's worth noting that year-end was two months ago. It's also worth noting that you can't agree this year's objectives until you've had your year-end review.

---

[92] This is to ensure the RAG status of the pointless KPI for the team for year-end reviews being complete reports as green on the corporate dashboard. Not only is it pointless but it also doesn't indicate that anyone has had a review. Just that they've filled in the paperwork.

You open the email to find someone who's been on one of your innovation training programmes has suggested you might be able to help on a project. The project lead has been tasked with creating some national health guidelines, which sound good in theory but are nigh on impossible to implement and get everyone to use. So they want to try a more innovative approach that might have a better chance of succeeding. Their first big challenge, they explain, is convincing the project board that something different is needed rather than repeating the standard approach that's typically taken.[93]

They sign off the email with 'Please say you can you help.'

---

[93] The standard approach for this type of project where national agreement is needed is to invite all stakeholders to attend a day-long 'collaboration' event where they're told what's needed before being asked for their views and opinions in various 'breakout sessions'. Oodles and oodles of sticky notes are used to capture these ideas on pieces of flipchart paper and attendees are thanked and assured this will all be reviewed and taken into account. The outputs are then folded up and taken back to the office where they'll gather dust behind someone's desk for two months before being ceremoniously dumped in the recycle bin by a disgruntled secretary. Someone will complain about this. Not about the fact that the ideas are going in the bin but that sticky notes can't be recycled and should therefore be put in the general rubbish bin. About a year later, the guidelines will emerge based on what people in offices think are good guidelines. They will, without exception, have failed to take into account real-life application and therefore be nigh on impossible to get implemented. Those at the original event will wonder why their ideas were ignored when they were so good and then do everything possible to make it impossible for the guidelines to gain any real traction. These events therefore achieve the opposite of what's needed (alignment) and also use up quite a lot of time and money. The only upside is the hot buffet.

You like a challenge so say, 'Yes, of course,' and suggest a call later that day to find out more.

During the call they explain a bit more about why it's so hard to get uptake for national guidelines.[94]

'Everyone knows that a top-down centralized approach that tries to tell a whole bunch of experts in their field what to do very rarely works and is often ignored,' they continue. 'And this particular project impacts across so many sectors and job roles that we don't see how it's remotely possible to have a one-off event with everyone present. But the expectation from the project board is that the team's key objective is to organize this event.'

'When do you next meet?' you ask.

'Two weeks,' they reply.

The team doesn't have any ideas what an alternative approach could be but want to try to persuade the project board to let them at least explore alternative approaches.

You suggest you get the team working virtually so you can get started quickly and introduce some of the new Ninja tools you've been learning to work at pace, especially as they're on the other side of the country and two weeks is, well, only two weeks away.

Current status ⏱ 78 ◐ 3

---

[94] See previous footnote.

Decision time

Do you:

a) Agree that you'll help the team to persuade the project board to run a more innovative 'event'? (page 155)

or

b) Persuade the team to persuade the project board group to not run the event but do something else entirely? (page 155)

This sounds like a big stakeholder management challenge. Not just for the 'event' itself but for the project board. Before you rush into a decision you decide to go and grab some lunch. You pick up Sami's Fables as you go – there might be some good advice you can pick up.

Sami's Fables Part 7

What a difference a name makes

Sami was in yet another of those workshops. This time it was for stakeholder mapping. It's something they had to do at the start of every project so someone could go away and write an engagement strategy.[95] Someone had drawn up a two-by-two grid on the wall and was asking everyone to write on sticky notes who the stakeholders were before asking how important or how much influence they had.

The facilitator was explaining that those in the high and high box would be communicated with the most. Sami was thinking how pointless this was but knew saying so wouldn't help. Sami remembered a story and started to work out how best to share it so that it could be useful.

---

[95] This was normally a list of ways to communicate (email, newsletters), how often these things would be done (weekly, monthly, etc.) and to which stakeholder groups. Nothing was mentioned about actual engagement and the list made little sense in relation to the project and what needed to be communicated but everyone felt good for having an engagement strategy.

When the list looked complete the facilitator asked whether there was anyone else they might have missed. This was Sami's chance.

'I'm not sure if we've captured everyone yet,' Sami offered. 'I wonder if the grid might be limiting our thinking though?'

'What do you mean?' the facilitator asked. 'This is the grid we always use.'

'Yes, I know,' said Sami, 'but can I share a story first?' The facilitator reluctantly agreed.

Sami then went on to talk about a project their friend had worked on. The project involved a big launch event, one of those with dignitaries and the press all turning up in their fancy clothes.

Great emphasis had been put on stakeholder engagement to ensure a smooth event. But, on the day itself, it was absolute chaos and all the plans fell apart. Why? Because none of the 'important' and 'influential' stakeholders turned up on time. Why? Because nobody, and I mean nobody, could get into the car park. Why? Because nobody had considered the car park attendant an important or influential stakeholder. In fact, no one had considered the car park attendant at all, so no one had engaged with him. They'd not even communicated with him. And this particular car park attendant was a real jobsworth.

No reservation, no access. He didn't care who they were.

Some of those in the room chuckled. They'd seen similar disasters in other projects.

'So, what would you suggest?' the facilitator asked, even more reluctantly.

Sami went on to explain that the work they'd done would be good for communication but not necessarily engagement. And that for success they needed to know who they needed to work with, names of real people, as this would determine what level of engagement was needed. Were these individuals in agreement with what they were trying to do? Did they understand it? Did they know what the expectations of them were?

'It's hard to guess these answers if we only identify groups of people,' Sami explained, 'but if we know *who* we need to deal with from, say, IT or HR, we can work out how best to get them on board as we're much more likely to have a sense of what they might think about the project. We can then tailor how we engage with those we need to make the project a success, like the car park attendant I mentioned.'

Sami explained that while 'we might have friends in HR, we might also have enemies. Knowing who exactly we'll need to engage with means we can try to work out in advance what they might think about our project.' Sami suggested that 'if the team worked out who might be fans of the project or who might not agree with what the team was doing they could develop specific ways of engaging with these individuals to get them on board'.

Sami stood up at the whiteboard and drew out a new stakeholder grid he had learned recently from the Prof, which plotted understand/don't understand against agree/don't agree and invited everyone to call out *actual* names of people they thought needed to be on board with the project and who they would need to rely on to do things.[96] The list was quite different and much more specific. And they quickly realized a lot of the individuals they'd identified were not in the friends box (agree with *and* understand the project). In fact, many were in the don't understand and don't agree box, which someone said was a tad worrying.

'Well yes,' said Sami, 'but if we focus on real engagement activities, and I don't mean sending them a newsletter but going to talk to them, then we can try to help them to understand what the change is about. They might still disagree, but we can then work with them to find out what specifically it is they disagree with. Rather than thinking they're being awkward, we might find out something important we don't yet

---

[96] Page 151 for template.

know. We can also perhaps use some of our friends as advocates to talk to their peers that are still not fully on board.'

This led to quite a lot of good discussion and the facilitator quickly started capturing some actions that were emerging.

Sami, for once, had got a point across without pissing everyone off. And it was leading to some good outputs that would be useful for the project. Sami thought that maybe, finally, they were becoming a bit Ninja at this stuff.

Ninja moves

Engage with *real* people

You can't engage with a department. Well, you can but it's a lot of work. Engaging is about real understanding, two-way involvement. This is why it's essential to separate communication and engagement. Telling someone about something doesn't mean you know what they think about it or that they'll do what you've told them they'll need to do. How often do you hear, 'Well I sent an email but they've not responded'?

People don't always say what they really mean. Think of any project or piece of work where someone you thought was in agreement has later tried to block what you're doing, or not done what you needed them to do. These are the people, the individuals you need to identify early, agree how you'll engage with them and put the effort into getting them on board with the project and making sure they know what's expected of them.

Next time you say, 'I'm going to engage with…' just ask yourself whether you are engaging, listening and understanding, or are you just telling them things (or sending an email) and assuming they agree because they haven't said they don't?

If you want to introduce new thinking and tools, ones that go against the norm, try using a story first, like the car park attendant. An example point makes it real and can be funny. It's also a way of creating group insight in a non-threatening manner, before introducing a new tool or approach.

Tools and templates

Don't forget the car park attendant

Don't just think about which group is most important and influential. Find out who you really need to make your project a success.

- Firstly, list all the actual people you think you need to engage with.
- Next decide whether they understand what you're doing and whether they agree with what you're doing.
- You'll need different ways to engage with those in each box.

Box a: People who understand your project... but seem to be against it for some reason. You need to find out why they don't agree. What do they know that you don't? Tackling them head on is unlikely to shift their thinking. Use IDQB™.[97]

---

[97] Remember when you used this with the Digital and Transformation Director to get access to an application download? The worst thing to do would have been going in and complaining about his team. The best thing to do was explain the issue and all the facts in a non-emotional way before asking a question that allowed you to work together on a solution. Page 106 for template.

StakeholderGrid2™

How do I get them (even the awkward ones) to engage?

People who seem to...

	Not agree with the goals of your project/change	Agree with the goals of your project/change
Understand what you are trying to achieve	a. Listen sincerely to their concerns and build them into your risks. Don't try to 'sell' to them.	b. Don't spend much time on this group. Just don't upset them.
Not understand what you are trying to achieve	c. Build trust. Get them to listen to the vision/approach (probably through a third party). Listen to their concerns.	d. Use an implications discussion to help them to recognise the impact of the change and become engaged.

Engaging Commitment

Copyright Eddie Obeng/Pentacle
All Rights Reserved
PENTACLETHEVBS.COM - QUBE.cc

Box b: You like these people. These are your friends. But make sure you don't spend all your time with them (which is hard not to do when they seem much easier to deal with). Also make sure you don't upset them (they're your advocates). Where you can, use them to 'win over' some of those in the other boxes.

Box c: You've heard that some people are having little digs about your project.[98] You know they don't really understand what it's about yet but still they're dismissing it. You need to spend some time with these individuals helping them understand the problem and why this project is so important. Ignore them at your peril. They'll continue to make digs about your project to others. Use the GapLeap™ with them.[99] Let them work through it. They may still disagree, but they're

---
[98] Let's call them the Blockers.
[99] Page 84.

much more likely to understand why the change needs to happen.

Box d: These are dangerous. You think they're fully on board. They're saying the right things, nodding and smiling. But do they really understand what you're doing? More importantly do they understand what they'll need to do and what they've committed to doing? Think back to a piece of work you've done where you thought *everyone* was on board, and then when you went to ask someone to do something they were either too busy to do it or would say things like 'well, I never agreed to do that'. With these individuals you need to make sure they know exactly what they're signing up for at the start by checking they understand the implications for them.

Using this stakeholder grid helps you:

- Identify *real* people to *engage* with *appropriately* rather than a one size fits all communication.
- Gives you a *real sense* of what *individuals might think* so you can plan how to get them on board.
- Help you *identify Blockers* early in the project to avoid a big project derail that may result in failure.

Your reflection

You take the last bite of your lunch and put the book down. You reflect on the conversation earlier about running a big stakeholder event and wonder which box all those stakeholders would fall into using this new grid (understand/don't understand, agree/don't agree).

And how impossible it would be to properly engage with them all in the different ways that would be needed to get them on board at one single event. But it gives you an idea…

Challenge 7

Continued...

Back to the challenge at hand. Remember, a team has asked you for help to persuade their project board to try an innovative approach to developing some national guidelines. Their first hurdle is to persuade the board that the traditional approach (bringing all stakeholders together and telling them the plans and asking their thoughts) never seems to work and is a waste of resources (time and money). They think, as a minimum, they should run a more innovative event that tries a more user-centred focus.

And you've been asked to help.

Decision time

Do you:

a) Agree that you'll help the team to persuade the project board to run a more innovative 'event'? (page 155)

or

b) Persuade the team to persuade the project board group to not run the event but do something else entirely? (page 155)

Agree that you'll help the team to persuade the project board to run a more innovative 'event'

You like a challenge. The team don't know what a user-centred event might look like but do ask whether you'll lead the design and facilitation on the day itself and you're flattered. You love creating things from scratch, especially where you have opportunities to try out new ideas.

Current status 🕐 72 ⓘ 3

But you could use up a lot of lifeline and health here.

Big events take a lot of hard work, time and effort. Traditional events fail to deliver the promises. What are the chances you could pull something off that really delivers what's needed? Especially given the complexity of this particular stakeholder group.

Current status 🕐 49 ⓘ 2

You know enough by now to know when to quit. You also know enough to be able to influence others in making the right choice based on their own insights.

You decide the team don't have a choice in this and you need to focus them on persuading the project board to try something entirely different.

Persuade the team to persuade the project board to not run the event but do something else entirely

Of course you do! The other option, running an event, even if it uses a very different approach, will still be the same old same old. It will burn a lot of resource (yours, the team, the participants), will cost a lot and is likely to fail on much-needed outcomes. What were you even thinking when you thought that was an option?

But you need to get the team to see that themselves first as it will give them the insights and confidence needed when talking to the board.

You suggest some further stakeholder analysis, remembering what you learned from Sami.

First, you get the team to list the stakeholder professions and organizations that will need to be persuaded to take up these new guidelines. They list over 50. That's 50 different organizations or professional groups that will need to be involved, ranging from surgeons to carers in the community. You all laugh at the thought of running an event for this number of differing views and opinions.

You then get the group to plot the 50 stakeholders not on importance and influence but in terms of how they might feel about this project.[100] Do they really understand it? Do they agree with it? You know this works better when you have actual names but for now this will, you think, make the point.

Not surprisingly the stakeholders are scattered all over the grid, with very few in the agree and understand camp.

You say to the team 'That's both a lot of stakeholders and a real mix in where they are in relation to

---

[100] Page 151 for template.

Challenge 7: Continued...

supporting this project. Are you now convinced that a big stakeholder event, however innovative, won't work?'

'Yes,' they all shout in unison. 'It's a crazy idea. But it's still unlikely the project board will agree, especially as we don't have any other ideas to suggest.'

You ask them which box they think the project board sit within in relation to doing something different and they decide it's the 'don't agree and don't understand' box.

You suggest that educating the board without telling them the answer is the way forward. 'That way, they'll come to the same conclusions you have by generating their own insights.'

'How will we do that?' the team ask.

'We just repeat what I did with you today,' you say.

Current status ☺ 83 ☻ 3

And two weeks later. Success!

You take the project board through the exact same process. All virtually so it doesn't take long and didn't need everyone to travel to a central location. After going through the same exercise, the reference group decides that a big event won't achieve what's needed (you've managed to move them into the agree and understand box) and they ask that the team goes away to explore other options.

You congratulate the team on getting what they wanted and explain that the best outcome is when someone else thinks it was their idea all along. 'Stealth-like moves,' you suggest, 'can be very effective.'

Over the next few weeks, the team meets once a week virtually, where you help them progress the project using many of the tools you've been learning about from Sami and the Prof, including Aladin-Journey™, to help with a user-design approach.[101]

Within a month, they've identified and scoped out a community-led approach. The idea is to ask different parts of the wider community to create their own guidelines that will be peer reviewed nationally before sign-off. Covering several communities, the team can then 'knit together' a national picture. Not only is this solution more likely to succeed given the users have designed it themselves but it also reduces the amount of work the core team needs to do as the users will be creating all the content. The team will instead focus on the platforms to host and share the content and ensure there's enough representation for peer reviewing the guidelines as they emerge.

Several weeks later the content is pouring in and the process is under way.

The team estimates they've saved around £50k of resources just from not running the event. They've also delivered outcomes many months ahead of schedule and have a delighted group of stakeholders who are engaged and supportive and acting as advocates for their peer group.

Current status ☯ 96 ☯ 3

You stop to reflect. This… this is exactly the type of thing you'd hoped to be doing when you started…

---

[101] Page 137 for template.

Helping teams think differently, creative problem-solving, but also saving time, money, energy, being more efficient, agile in approaches, motivating teams – in short, transforming ways of working. It might be innovation with a small 'i' but it's still innovation. It doesn't need to be huge to be different and effective. This is a good baseline/case study for trying to scale up this way of working, you think. And off you go to tell lots of other people about it.

Challenge 8

Too serious to play

Here we go again, you think as you come off the phone.

Someone just called you in a bit of a panic. Can you help? They need to run a two-day workshop for 40 high-level professionals. The dates are in the calendar and it's in three weeks' time. There's no venue yet, no facilitator yet and no real plan yet. But they're adamant that the event needs to cover a list of 'things' they think it needs to cover because that list of things was included in the invite and it's 'what people will expect'.

You carefully point out that the things on the list are really already answers to questions rather than problem statements that need to be addressed. You also suggest that as the workshop is being sold as a collaborative event to identify some answers to key questions, then it could be seen by the participants as a futile exercise if they perceive that someone has already agreed what the answers are. But they're adamant it has to be this way.[102]

'But,' they plead, 'can you please help?'

It's a high-profile workshop with outcomes feeding into a national strategic agenda. Engagement and participation needs to be high.

You've been here before... drafted in with little time to design and prepare and it's not as if you'd have been twiddling your thumbs over the next three weeks and you do have a pretty full schedule already.[103] When drafted in with little say over the already issued agenda, often as not you'll say yes in the vain hope you can rescue what could be a disaster. Often as not, you end up looking like a bad facilitator when it does, indeed, go pear-shaped because, despite your protests, the sponsors will still insist on doing it their way.

Decision time

Do you:

a) Say you'd love to help but unfortunately just can't fit it in? (page 162)

or

---

[102] As they always are. Even when the logic is *seriously* flawed.

[103] It seems to be a common expectation of internally run workshops that you can just rock up on the day and 'facilitate'. Little, nay zero, thought is given to design and preparation time. Unless, that is, they bring in someone externally. Then they're willing to pay the big bucks to invest in design over several weeks, months even. Because they're experts.

b) Say yes, because you're rubbish at saying no, and you think maybe, just maybe, this time I can persuade them otherwise? (page 163)

Say you'd love to help but unfortunately just can't fit it in

This isn't a bad idea. In fact, it's a very very good idea. It will be a lot of hard work, banging your head against a wall and you're unlikely to be able to steer them fully in the way that's needed. At best it might turn out to be okayish, with participants feeling they've either been consulted with or at least asked for their views.

But even then you know nothing really will happen as a result, so in reality it's a lot of resources down the drain (40-plus highly paid staff for two days at an external venue).[104] Also, if you say no you won't find yourself in a compromised position looking like a bad facilitator at the front with a flipchart and pen should it go, nay, when it goes pear-shaped.

Current status ☻ 83 ☺ 3

But...

Are you letting them down? They'll run the event regardless. And it could end up much, much worse if they don't get any pushback from whoever they draft in to lead. It could end up a real car wreck if they can't get a proper facilitator.

Current status ☻ 63 ☺ 2

---

[104] With the expected hot buffet.

And, also, this is part of a huge national strategy. A strategy that really needs people to be thinking differently. And you know that you can't keep complaining about all the things that are wrong with the system if you don't at least try to make some changes, however small. Are you starting to give up or think maybe it's time to move on?

Current status ◐ 43 ◑ 1

If you still want to say no head to page 23… but if you think you're too far into this journey and still think you can and want to make a difference, however small, then cast aside those small niggling doubts (okay so they aren't so small and they're very, very real) and read on.

Say yes because you're rubbish at saying no, and you think maybe, just maybe, this time I can persuade them otherwise

Yes, yes, yes, you know you're rubbish at saying no. But this is a big one. It could be an opportunity to try to change the how, the thinking, the being, the doing with a group of fairly senior staff. So, you say yes on the condition that they support you in using some new tools to help shift thinking. You also insist that the space has to be right for the event and you'll not do it in a squashed-up boardroom or a sterile hotel meeting room with no space to properly workshop.

So the event is planned and a venue procured. Due to the last-minute nature there's little choice, so you end up at the zoo… in the middle of the bonobo enclosure. And yes, you'll have chimps watching you work all day.[105]

Based on the desired outcomes, you suggest, nay insist on using LEGO® Serious Play® (LSP)... it's one of the most effective, inclusive and powerful workshop tools you've come across for shifting thinking, working collaboratively, creating new ideas and getting people aligned. It's a tool that makes it really hard for people to disengage from and, so far, you've only ever had successful outcomes when using it.

The sponsor is sceptical. They're not convinced the participants will go for it. You promise it will give them some real results and that you'll do the 'science' of why it works to help convince the participants to give it a try.

The LEGO® is ordered at great pain (no one is happy to sign off on procuring a 'toy') but finally you're good to go.

You set the room up the night before. Forty participants, one facilitator, introducing a new method and some pre-agreed answers to consult on.[106] What could go wrong?

Current status ☿ 65 ◐ 3

---

[105] And there will be the bonobos in the bonobo enclosure watching you all day too. Boom boom!

[106] You've at least managed to prep six tabletop facilitators to help manage the groups. It never matters how much you insist that one facilitator for 40 attendees is a huge risk if they want good outputs. They never budge. Because they still think you're just the person with the flipchart pen capturing things on flipchart paper.

Day one and participants start to arrive. You can hear complaints already about the location and the obvious signs of LEGO®.[107]

You introduce the session and spend a good amount of time on the science behind how and why LSP works. These are, after all, scientists, so can generally be persuaded when presented with research and facts.

You feel their mood shift a little and go on to explain the agenda for the day. First to learn the LSP method through a series of guided exercises before building a shared model, in collaboration, to a challenge question.[108] They (reluctantly) agree to give it a go. They learn the method before being presented with the challenge question. They then build their individual answer to this question before being asked to work, in teams, to build a shared response to the question. A shared build that should reflect everyone's views on what this future organization should look like.

---

[107] It's probably a good time to point out that the participants aren't quite fully behind this big national strategy as the likelihood is they'll be impacted directly and they're not keen on change. That's what the workshop is about really. To get them to come up with what they'd like the future to look like. But they really don't like change and think everything is just fine and dandy as it is. You did have an idea that this might be the case but nobody had warned you just how disgruntled they might be.

[108] In this instance the challenge questions are along the lines of what this new future organization should look like from their particular aspect/area of expertise in terms of services and attributes and what they would need to do to achieve it.

Pretty soon into the shared build you notice they're not really engaged in the process or interested in collaborating or generating new ideas. They just want it over with. There's discussion, but it's all very negative and in some cases it's quite aggressive and dismissive of each other's views. One person has built a big brick wall and they're trying to hide behind it. No one on the table has asked them if they're okay as they're too busy battling with their neighbour. One group say they can't respond to the question as they weren't mentioned, as a group of experts, in a recent publication, so therefore they don't exist.[109]

The tabletop facilitators don't know what to do. You've haven't prepared them for conflict resolution. But by the end of the day, each table has built a shared model to answer the challenge question they were given, and each table tells the story of what their model represents. And it's bad.[110] It's worse than bad. It's terrible. And it really doesn't lend itself well to the planned activities for the next day.

---

[109] You ask them whether writing their specialism down on a piece of paper would make a difference. They say yes, of course it would. These are senior experts in their field throwing their toys out of the pram because they weren't mentioned specifically in a short, for the general public, communication. A public who, in the main, wouldn't really understand what this specialist role was.

[110] The stories mostly consist of buzzword bingo words such as transparency, collaboration and innovation but are empty and meaningless stories and tell nothing of what needs to happen to make these things so.

Challenge 8: Too serious to play

At the end of the day, the core team has a wash-up and you all agree you need to replan the second day. You're up until 10pm that night frantically redesigning the next day's activities before a not very good sleep.

Current status ⏱ 47 ♥ 2

It's day two. The participants are even more reluctant to be there. You introduce the plan for the day. It's essentially a disguised rerun of the previous day with a different context setting around it in the hope this will stimulate creative thinking.

There's outrage.

'We did that yesterday…'

'It doesn't work…'

'What's the point?'

'No one is going to listen to our suggestions…'

'None of us want this change…'

'How can we come up with ideas when we don't even know who our managers are going to be?'

This last one throws you slightly as it really shouldn't matter, but you can see that they're really quite angry.

Then they start arguing with each other.[111]

You look at the sponsor, who's most definitely not making eye contact with you and is most definitely gazing at the bonobos eating broccoli.

---

[111] It's a bit like that bit in *The Life of Brian* when they're arguing about whether they should be called the People's Front of Judea or the Judean People's Front.

You follow his gaze. The broccoli-munching bonobos are looking at you and seem to be shrugging with disbelief. It's a tad disconcerting.

Current status 🕐 39 ◐ 2

Decision time

Do you:

a) Panic? (page 168)

or

b) Develop superhuman powers? (page 169)

Panic

Well, it's an option and the first one that springs to mind. You tell yourself you knew this would happen and yet again you've been put in an impossible compromising position. You shouldn't be on your own with this many people, the sponsor should have listened to you about content – you know, that first big risk you pointed out about the list of things they insisted on including that you knew the participants would read as 'everything's all already been agreed so why are you bothering to ask us now?'

And you had also suspected there would be another elephant in the room. The elephant being that the participants didn't want to be there because they were against the big proposed changes full stop. When you'd suggested you spent time teasing some of this out you were told no, that wasn't part of the agenda for the event. And so here you are and you're not sure what to do.

Current status ⊙ 31 ◐ 1

But you can do this. It's time to create superhuman powers.

Develop superhuman powers

You take a big breath. Time slows down to let you plan.[112]

Step 1) You're not going to panic.

Step 2) You're going to keep your cool and stay composed. This is not your doing.

Step 3) You have the tools and the confidence to deal with this. The Prof is right behind you whispering you're a Ninja. Remember StakeholderGrid2.[113] This group probably understand what you're trying to do but just don't agree. The best tool for this group is IDQB™ (share the issue, data and ask them a question before building the solution together).[114]

Current status ⊙ 41 ◐ 2

Step 4) Firmly tell yourself that maybe you really should listen to your instincts more. There was an option to say no to this event and you chose to ignore it.

---

[112] This is your superhuman power I mentioned at the start. To slow time down to give you time to think when needed. It feels as if you've hit the pause button on the room.

[113] Page 151 for template.

[114] Page 106 for template.

Step 5) Don't overthink it. Don't defend what you're trying to do.

'Okay,' you say.[115] 'You don't want to do what I've suggested and that's okay. This is your day; this is an expensive day in relation to your time. And this is a day where *you* have the opportunity to produce a plan for a future *you* want. We tried that yesterday and didn't get very far so we thought we could try a different way to get your ideas today, but you don't like that plan either.[116] Tell me what you'd like to do. We'll break for tea, and I'll redesign the rest of the day.'

After some discussion amongst themselves and some low-level grumbling they collectively fold their arms and agree to do what you'd suggested in the first place.[117]

Current status ⏱ 52 ◐ 2

And they do the LEGO® build again in response to pretty much the same challenge question that's just been pitched in a different context. Not only do they do it again, but they do it well. Really well. They collaborate with each other, particularly with those from different organizations who they completely dismissed the day before. New conversations are sparking, they're asking you questions about things they think you can

---

[115] Releasing the pause button.

[116] You know they have plenty of ideas. They're just being stubborn and think by being stubborn they might 'win' and get what they really want, which is to maintain the status quo.

[117] Kerching... *A very nice Ninja move*, you tell yourself. The Prof would be proud.

Challenge 8: Too serious to play 171

help with, new ideas are forming, follow-up meetings are being arranged.

As you wander around listening in you can't believe this is the same group as yesterday. You assume it's in part because they didn't have any other suggestions but also in part because they made themselves look a bit foolish, which has made them a bit sheepish. You'll need to reflect on this properly later as there's probably something else going on too.

The room is buzzing with new opportunities and possibilities. By lunchtime, each table has a video of their aligned story, their response to the challenge question that was set. There's a collective sigh of relief from the core team as the participants head into the zoo for a well-earned lunch break.

You take some time to reflect. This is a group of highly professional experts who should be able to work collaboratively and influence their own future. You know a lot of these individuals, and on a one-to-one level they're great. But as a group they're trapped in a particular culture that dictates how they behave. And the only time they truly align is when they feel, as a group, that they're under attack. This culture means they always respond the way they think they're meant to.[118] It's a great example of group think and group do.

Giving them space and time to express their feelings about these two days was crucial. Holding a mirror up to them so they could see how they were

---

[118] Generally, arms folded and minds closed against anything they feel they're being told they must do.

behaving was also needed before they could relax their guard.[119] This was all needed before they would give themselves permission to respond as individuals and not as a group forming a protective barrier. Once they'd done that, they could really engage in the process and bring their own insights and thoughts to the challenge at hand. Only then were they open to collaborating on new ideas.

Current status 🕐 68 💧 3

On a personal note, you resolve to never put yourself in this position again. A position where you'll be compromised based on someone else's thinking and behaviours. It's time, you think, to start thinking about a new adventure…

Oh, and the event itself becomes quite infamous and is forever known in hushed tones as 'that event at the zoo'.

Current status 🕐 91 💧 3

Phew. You survived another day. But blimey this is hard work. You're still chuckling about the bonobos though. It couldn't have been a more perfect venue. But you're starting to get weary of being put in compromising situations, and although you think you're getting better at saying no, the reality is that you mostly think you can make Ninja moves, swoop in and fix things and so tend to say yes.

---

[119] You now always add at least 30 minutes to any workshop design as a 'just in case' for dealing with elephants in the room. If you're using LEGO® you just get them to build the issue and they mostly end up working it all out themselves as the tool makes it feel safe to do so.

Challenge 8: Too serious to play

What a lot of learning in the last year or so, though. The tools are starting to become second nature. You know not to react but try to see the Blockers as individuals and work out where they are in their head before selecting the right tool to help them gain insights and shift their thinking. It might feel slow at times and it's frustrating, but by doing so you've been able to make progress, by stealth, to achieve some great outcomes.

You wonder what you've not yet mastered, so you grab a cuppa and pull out your now very tattered copy of Sami's Fables.

Sami's Fables Part 8

Sami was at a team meeting. The team were painstakingly going through the risk log, which to be fair wasn't as long as it could have been. Someone else notices this but, rather than celebrate that they as a team were perhaps getting better at doing things to minimize risk, it was suggested that perhaps they should do an audit on risk numbers on average for, say, the last five years. You know, to see if it's lower than it should be, in which case the team might want to think about what other risks there might be. Everyone agreed that this was an action that should be done. Sami mentally banged their head against a brick wall.

They moved on to the next risk on the risk log. Sami noticed the date it had been raised was ten years ago. *Ten* years. Sami suggested that perhaps it wasn't really a risk they could do anything about if it hadn't been dealt with yet and maybe it should be closed. This wasn't agreed by everybody. It wasn't agreed by anybody.

The risk lead then made a point of it being a real risk by reading it out. 'There's a risk that due to data servers being directly under a flight path we could, in the event of an aircraft accident, lose all of our data.'

Sami thought that if this were a real risk then the obvious fix would have been to move the servers somewhere else.[120] But that action is nowhere to be seen in the mitigation plan. In fact, no actions are listed anywhere in the mitigation plan because other than moving them there's not much that can be done. And that's why it was still open after ten years.

'But wait a minute,' Sami spoke up. Sami had a cunning plan to get this risk closed. There were real risks that needed real action and they'd never get to them at this rate. 'The servers are just over the road, aren't they? Only a couple of hundred metres away.'

'And your point?' asked the risk lead wearily.

'Well doesn't that mean that there's also a risk that we lose all of our staff and office in the event of an aircraft accident as we too are under the flight path. Is there a risk logged for that?'

Sami immediately sensed this had been a mistake and remembered, too late, that pointing out obvious flaws in logic never went down well.

---

[120] Maybe nine-and-a-half years ago.

The chair decided they'd leave risk for now and come back to it next time as there were other things to do, and they only had ten minutes left.

Typically, once Sami had stopped feeling so frustrated, Sami remembered the alien story the Prof had shared just the other week. Aliens were, it seemed, a great way to manage risk – actually manage risk, not just manage the process of managing risks.[121]

It started with a general question about 3x3 or 5x5 risk-scoring matrices (the likelihood of something happening against the impact it would have). Everyone in the session agreed this was standard risk management process.

'And then everything gets a colour, right? A RAG status?' the Prof had continued. Everyone nodded.

'Red means danger, so you make the risk red to indicate you need help but instead you're told off for not managing the project properly and told to go and sort it out before the next meeting. So next time, you're clever. You make the risk green. But instead of the "well done" you expected for managing it from red to green. Nothing. Because no one ever looks at green risks, so no one even noticed what you'd done. So next time you aim for amber. Am I still on track?'

---

[121] Which is what most of risk management seemed to be. At least to Sami.

Everyone nodded, some glumly, but many smiling. How ridiculous it sounded when said out loud, Sami thought. But it was so spot on.

'So, you have your big spreadsheet with all this information about risk, and mitigation plans, and proximity dates, and coded by type of risk and where 90% are shaded amber. And this is important because these are the things that are going to throw your project off track if they happen, right?'

Everyone nods.

'Now hands up if you always *start* a meeting focusing on trying to get rid of the risks, and if you do nothing else you put in place real actions, you'll do immediately to get rid of the risks?'

Sami glanced around. There were no hands up.

The Prof continued. 'Okay, so when you do get to the risk bit, how much time do you spend on actually fixing the risks versus talking about mitigation plans and type of risk and when the risk might happen, to make sure all the boxes on your spreadsheet are filled in? I'm guessing not much. When did you last add actions from a risk review meeting to your project plan? Isn't that what the plan is for? The things you need to do to deliver? I'm guessing not often. Am I still on track?'

Again, lots of nodding.

'So, you see, very few people actually manage risks, but they spend an awful lot of time discussing and managing the process of risks. But don't worry. I have a secret to share that will make you all risk management gurus.'

He then went on to talking about alien films.

'Think about alien films,' he continued.

'Now, think what happens in them. An alien rocks up, a small team, two or three people, go out to kill the alien, and before long they get to a junction and decide to split up. Bad mistake. One of them is devoured by said alien and all you get is the crackle of static on their walkie talkie.

'Next, a second team goes out. There are more of them, they have better weapons and they stick together. After a lot of stop and start music they finally catch said alien, take it back to the lab and lock it up for the night before heading off to celebrate.

'Jim, it's always Jim, is left in charge of said alien and falls asleep/plays too many video games/smokes the wrong type of cigarette, allowing the alien to escape. Jim gets eaten, the alien squelches off and ends up making lots of baby aliens, lots and lots of baby aliens, which appear everywhere doing untold damage. The aliens start to take over to such an extent that the only option is to blow up the planet/spaceship.

'Think about it. Every alien film. We can therefore conclude that Hollywood has taught us how to manage risk by showing us what *not* to do.

'Think of risks as aliens: 1. Identify the alien; 2. Kill the alien dead. And don't split up. Ever; 3. Contain the alien. Don't leave Jim in charge; 4. If it escapes, monitor it to see where those baby aliens are; and 5. Have a plan B to blow up the planet/spacecraft.

'Every time you identify an alien, work through each step to come up with actions. Then do the "kill it" action to get rid of the risk. You'll find you mostly kill them dead straight up. You can use my Fix-It-NOW™ tool to work through this.'[122]

Sami wondered whether this story would have worked on the team at the meeting. Probably not, Sami reflected, feeling a little better. Probably not.

---

[122] Page 182 for template.

Ninja moves

Is it process for process's sake or is it adding real value?

This is not unlike the business continuity exercise. Long long ago, someone somewhere wrote in a book that these types of things are a good thing to do. Business continuity plans, risk management, benefits management, highlight reports. And someone, somewhere, agreed they did indeed sound like good things to do because they make sense to do, don't they? If you want to deliver successful change.

But at some point between those processes being put in place and those processes being mandated, the real purpose of them was lost. The real rich content that made sense and how that content was acted on was lost. When was the last time you said 'we have a risk' and everyone jumped up and said 'let's focus on how we can fix it and put actions in place to get rid of it, and what can I do to help?' Or the last time you shared a highlight report and everyone said 'well done but really we should be focusing on what we're doing next rather than what happened last month'? Or the last time you were all sent home to test the business continuity plan in the event that the office couldn't open?

So, over time, much of this good stuff has just become a paper exercise that burns up time and sucks out your soul. And this is what needs to change. But it's so ingrained it needs Ninja moves, stealth-like action that no one notices until they realize things suddenly seem much better and that the improvement was all down to them. You might not get the credit but, remember, to be a Change Ninja you also need to demonstrate invisible leadership.

Tell stories as you go, use the tools in this book and things will start to shift. And everyone loves an alien story.

Tools and templates

Aliens and UFOs

Remember, risk management should be about just that and not about managing the risk management process. And if you think of risks as aliens and then aim to kill them *now* you'll end up managing risks and not worrying too much about the process.

Fix-It-NOW™ — Surviving the Aliens

	Fears/Risks (at the start)	Fix-It-NOW!	Containment Actions	Fears/Risks (still left)	Monitoring <Fears/Risks still left only>	Contingency or Plan B
Your point of view...						
Their point of view...						
	1. IDENTIFY THE DANGER	2. KILL IT NOW!	3. LIMIT IT/ CONTAIN IT	IF YOU'RE SAFE RELAX OR...	4. KEEP AN EYE ON IT	5. IF ALL PLANS FAIL - NOW WHAT?

Title/ Objective _____

Copyright Eddie Obeng/Pentacle
All Rights Reserved
PENTACLETHEVBS.COM – QUBE.cc
PENTACLE

- Identify the risk (alien).
- Kill it now (don't split up).
- Contain it (don't leave the wrong person in charge that lets it escape).
- What risk might be left?
- How will you monitor the remaining risk (to see if it's multiplying)?
- What's your plan B (blow up the planet)?
- Work through each box for your identified risk. Put the kill it now action into your project plan/action list and action it.

What are you waiting for? *Fix it now.*

Reflection

You look back to that workshop with the LEGO® and the badly behaved chimps. You wonder whether carrying out a Fix-It-NOW™ on saying yes or the workshop design would have helped, particularly with day one. Yes, you think. It would have helped enormously. If you'd identified the alien – that the sponsors were mostly going through the motion of being seen to run the sessions rather than being fully engaged in wanting to see a great outcome – you'd have tried to kill it. If you'd identified the alien – that the participants felt devalued and had no intention of 'engaging' in the process – you might not have been able to kill it but could have contained it better.

By working through this process you could have put things in place that may have prevented the huge derail. But these types of risks were never really thought of whenever risk management came up. The real risks, the ones about people, behaviours and intent. But still. You got to use your superhuman strength of stopping time, which had to be worth something. *What next?* you wonder. *What next?*

Challenge 9

Beating the drum

You're feeling a bit flat. You've found a way of working that has meant you can do a lot more value-added activity. You managed to get rid of lots of the valueless time-wasting and energy-draining tasks, such as meaningless meeting agendas, writing papers that either no one reads or are full of endless tracked changes rendering the document unreadable. You no longer need Doodle poll to align diaries (which are out of date as soon as you send them), someone to take detailed minutes (so you can check at the next meeting that they're indeed an accurate reflection of a past conversation about past activities). You no longer need everyone on the team to be there at the same time before you can progress anything (and hardly ever is everyone there at the same time).

Challenge 9: Beating the drum

If you're eager to know how and want to short cut the next story, then jump to page 193 and take Sami's Quiz. You can always come back again.

Current status ☠ 51 ⦿ 3

You and a few other pirates you regularly work with have managed to do quite a few of those things that were on those A3 sheets at the far end of the boardroom at that very first workshop (agile, innovation, empowered, transformation). But not everyone has engaged with how you've managed it, particularly those that are in a position to really champion and help scale up what you're doing.[123] In fact, some of them are actively trying to block what you're doing. And yes, you've done quite a lot of the IDQB™s and stakeholder management grids but this is bigger than that. They just don't seem to like the 'idea' of this virtual,[124] non-hierarchical,[125] empowering, no-nonsense way of working.

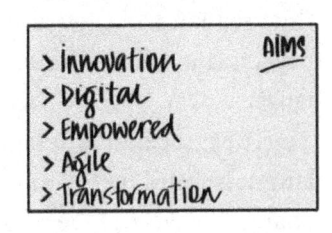

> AIMS
> > Innovation
> > Digital
> > Empowered
> > Agile
> > Transformation

---

[123] Mini Cheddars, Steely Governance Manager, Digital Transformation Director and the Blockers. Oh so many Blockers.

[124] Remember, this is pre-Covid where virtual was mostly an exception, and access to digital solutions was far from universal. When VC meetings did take place, they tended to be between two or three offices and lose 20 minutes of the meeting trying to get sound to work.

[125] Non-hierarchical in the old VC worlds tended to be Jim or Maya craning their necks to try to be in the line of the video, which was fixed on the wall and unable to get everyone sitting round the table in the picture.

'It's not the same as meeting face to face,' they'll say, or, 'I really like to see the whites of people's eyes and you can't do that virtually.'[126] This reveals more about their old-world management and leadership style than they realize and they don't see the irony of this as they preach the values of inclusiveness, empowerment and trust.

They also complain about not seeing body language and yet you've never noticed a manager change what they're doing when, for example, the room is full of bored, disengaged or disgruntled body language. You've only seen it being used as a weapon to admonish somebody. Again, not really in line with the organizational values.

People are shocked that you've stopped automatically writing things up as formal documents even though you have a saved copy of what everyone has written directly on to the tools you've introduced.[127]

'What about governance?' they ask. But when you question what this means, no one can give you an answer or explain what the risk of, say, not writing a formal paper would mean. So, what might be an actual need for some documentation for some things has, over time, become a perceived need for everything 'just in case'.[128]

---

[126] You're not entirely sure how this aligns with the organizational values, but often senior managers feel they're exempt from such values.

[127] And where the tools have a framework in the background, so the content is instantly understandable.

[128] More process for process's sake.

Challenge 9: Beating the drum

You also get fed up with the Blockers' regular comments along the lines of: 'Yes it would be great, and I'd love to give what you're doing a go but I'm pretty sure my team won't like it,' or 'I really don't have time to try anything new, even if it will save me time.'[129] Their arrogant assumption that while, yes, they're up for it and smart enough for it, but it might just be a bit too much for the people they manage or that they're too important to even contemplate reprioritizing their workload to try to improve how they work.

And the worst comment you hear of all is, 'That sort of thing just doesn't work,' from the Blockers who've never done anything different, ever, and are 'far too busy to be playing around with things that just don't work' if you offer them a demo and some facilitation in these new tools. And these are the people who all have roles in their respective areas for leading change and transformation.

Current status 🕐 37 ☻ 2

But… word has got out. The viral spread of good ideas is starting to work for some teams.[130]

'What are these tools you're using?' 'What do you mean they make people and teams more efficient?' 'How can you even get rid of unnecessary meetings and papers?' 'What do you mean you hardly get email anymore?' 'What is this witchcraft?'

---

[129] There's a great cartoon of two cavemen trying to move a cart with square wheels. Someone offers them a round wheel and they dismiss it, saying they don't have time. You realize you work with a lot of cavemen.

[130] Pre-Covid viral spread didn't sound quite as scary as it does now!

These are questions you're getting asked more and more. The curiosity and positive feedback make you feel better. Staff are starting to become curious, and your original plan was always small fires burning and organic spread, so it's not all bad.

Current status ⏱ 52 ⓘ 2

Decision time

Do you:

a) Think maybe this will only ever be a small solution for a select few? (page 188)

or

b) Keep trying – you know it could transform a huge chunk of everyday working? (page 189)

Think maybe this will only ever be a small solution for a select few

And you're quite possibly right. While it should work for everyone, would change behaviours and process, make everything much more agile, inclusive and efficient, meet the carbon reduction KPI, give staff more choice in how and where they work, free up time from doing pointless work about work to focus on real problem-solving and development of creative solutions… it's probably just too much too soon.

You're not giving up exactly. But you're giving up the big fight. It's no longer worth it. Nobody really wants this change they're talking about. It might be time to start thinking about other areas to invest your energy in.

Current status 🕐 32 ⓞ 1

Decision time

Do you:

a) Stop fighting and think I need to move on? (page 23)

or

b) Keep trying – you know it could transform a huge chunk of everyday working? (page 189)

Keep trying – you know it could transform a huge chunk of everyday working

Of course you do.

You've transformed how you work and as a result are so much happier. Not just because you're doing something you love but you've managed to get rid of so much work that's just about work.[131] Now you spend most of your time doing activities that directly lead to outcomes. You hardly ever go to (dull and pointless) meetings. Hardly ever write papers that will just gather dust. You work at home when you can. Have started

---

[131] You recently came across Dave Graeber's Bullshit jobs essay, so much of which resonated. www.davidgraeber.org

running at lunchtime or taking the dogs for a good walk, and curiously have found that this is a much better way to produce ideas for the latest problem rather than staring at the computer screen.[132]

And after a few days off, with a little self-indulgence, you come back into the office determined to keep raising awareness, keep challenging the status quo, knowing you'll need to keep banging your head against the wall on a frequent basis.

Current status 🕐 64 🍎 2

Three things happen about the same time:

- A bunch of random staff members want a taste of this sorcery. 'We want what you have,' they clamour.

- A team who are desperate to progress some work, but wary of what that might mean for them in terms of time and effort, are also very keen to explore this urban myth of a six-week project.

- Some very smart people know they need to come together to solve a problem but: a) they're very busy smart people; and b) they can't quite agree what the real problem is but are willing to let you have a go at getting them where they need to be.

Current status 🕐 71 🍎 2

---

[132] But also know that no one would consider this real work.

Challenge 9: Beating the drum

Before you respond to any of this you want to reflect a bit more on this new way of working. You know Sami has probably described it in a useful way that you could share and use with these new requests for help.

Sami's Fables Part 9

Sami was reflecting on all the new learning and new tools they'd been applying, sharing and teaching others how to use. Some areas and teams had really embraced this new way of working and there were clear benefits. But there was still some reluctance and still many Blockers making excuses by saying 'that's not how we do things' or using 'governance' as a reason to carry on doing things the same old, same old way.

Despite all the organizational strategies and visions for a transformed, digital workplace, many seemed quite happy just carrying on doing what they'd always done. Even if they were working on digital or transformative projects, the way they were doing it was the traditional way with meeting after meeting, paper after paper and slow, slow progress. If Sami challenged this, then the one big innovation project would get mentioned as a success story.[133] Every time.

---

[133] Shiny gadget.

There was very little learning or willingness to try to do things differently, yet the expectation was that the results would be different. Sami and those Sami worked with had transformed how they worked using these new tools and approaches. There were plenty of stories of delivering projects in just six to eight weeks rather than the typical six-month minimum. And it wasn't a case of just putting more hours in, the teams reported that they were spending less time on a weekly basis on these projects than other traditionally run projects.

Sami thought it might be useful to share this knowledge more widely. But how to raise the profile so that people might actually apply the learning and use the tools? There were already so many best practice guides, toolkits and 'play books' that just gathered dust. So, Sami, who now knew to test ideas on the intended audience before doing all the work, used the human-centred design approach to gather insights on how this could be done. The result was a 'Do things different to do different things' quiz.

Do things different to do different things quiz rules

Read each section, scoring yourself as you go for anything you routinely do. Score -20 points for everything you do in the 'traditional' column. Score +20 points for everything you do in 'transformed working' column.

All the tools mentioned in the transformed working column can be found throughout the book and in the appendix.

You can cheat if you want to. But cheating won't actually help you deliver your change any quicker or make your team any happier.

Round 1 – Stop looking in the rear-view mirror and focus on what's in front of you	
Traditional	**Transformed working**
Team meeting:	Team meeting: Don't send an agenda. (+20)
Set agenda, send two weeks in advance, often send the exact same agenda every time if it's a recurring meeting. (-20) Spend a large proportion of the meeting getting updates from everyone on what they've done since the last meeting, often in the form of highlight reports you've spent some time writing. (-20)	No agenda you ask? But how will we know what the meeting is about?[134] Here's what to do instead: At the start of the 'meeting' ask for everyone's 'hopes and fears'.[135] Get rid of the fears first by de-risking them. This helps manage any elephants in the room

---

[134] Before you insist on an agenda, ask yourselves this. Does a typical standard agenda give you real insight into why you're having a meeting? What's its real purpose? What are the intended outcomes? What decisions need to be made and why is your presence needed? And if you don't know all this, how often do you go anyway? And if you do go, how often do you think, well… that was a waste of time? Many meeting agendas don't set out clear purpose or desired outcomes, so they can become talking shops about the things the agenda setter thought you all needed to talk about.

[135] Page 208 for a template.

Anything extra such as 'eek' things we need to discuss and make decisions on can be raised under AOCB.[136] (-20)	or latest project catastrophe first so you can agree actions to resolve them (remember the aliens). (+20)
AOCB comes at the end of the agenda and typically about three minutes before the end of the meeting, following the agenda item about risk. That is, when everyone is bored beyond belief or rushing off to their next meeting, irrelevant of whether your business is competent or not.[137] (-20)	The team will now feel safe and supported in raising such concerns in the future. (+20)
	Then organize the hopes into an order that makes sense. Read through them and ask everyone one by one whether this makes sense as the agenda for today's meeting. *Et voila* – you have an agenda that reflects what needs doing and the team are aligned on this agenda. (+20)
Real things don't get discussed, so progress is delayed until the next meeting, when you try to get the real thing added to the standard agenda. (-20)	Next, spend the rest of the meeting working on these items to progress the project and not just talk about it. For example, if mapping stakeholders comes up as a hope, then work as a team on doing this in the meeting rather than discussing it and assigning it for someone to do outside the meeting. (+20)
	Et voila – the project has moved forward. (+20)
Round 1 score – how did you do?	
Total points available: (-100)	Total points available: (+120)

---

[136] Any Other Competent Business. Incompetent business doesn't get a look-in. Sami is not sure this is always true though.

[137] If ever there was an agenda item to suck the life out of a meeting it's going over the risk register.

Round 2 – Project briefs vs Brief projects	
Traditional	**Transformed working**
Call a traditional meeting to discuss a new project and all talk for an hour on what you think it is. (-20)	Get the team together face to face, virtual or a mix.
	Do a Hopes&Fears™ to align the team. (+20)
Ask the project manager in the room (or the person you think should manage the project, irrelevant of skills and experience) to go away and write a project brief. If you're feeling optimistic make it a project initiation document. (-20)	Maybe provide some background on *why* you've gathered the team then use the 5Ps™ tool (Purpose, Principles, People, Process, Performance) to find out what others think it's all about, by adding sticky notes to each of the 5Ps™.[139] (+20)
The volunteered project manager will then head to a metaphorical dark cupboard under the stairs to 'write a project brief' in isolation before emerging slightly pasty-faced several weeks later with a first draft (v0.1).[138] (-20)	Write before you speak.[140] (+20)
	Order the stickies to tell a story and read through it. Check in with the team one by one to check they're happy with it.[141] (+20)

---

[138] Now on referred to as PFPM – pasty-faced project manager.

[139] Page 50 for a template.

[140] This always works better virtually, as when you're in a room together the tendency is to discuss first, which can very quickly lead to group think. But it can still be done, with practice, in face-to-face sessions to ensure diversity, inclusivity, sharing of new ideas, capturing of quiet people's views. All those things that are talked about on leadership training programmes but often not really put into action well.

[141] It's called SpinCasting™. Just ask everyone individually: Does this work for you? Go round the table or do it alphabetically so everyone knows when they're next in the list.

This is then discussed at length in the next meeting, where the PFPM is largely ignored before the brief is distributed for further comments. (-20)	Fifteen minutes later you'll have an outline project brief, which can also be used as a summary that can be used to communicate wider what the project is about and what outcomes (rather than outputs) you're trying to achieve so the team is clear what success looks like. You'll also have an idea of who else you might need to bring into the team. (+20)
Everyone eventually responds individually with their own tracked changes that the PFPM has to merge. The second draft appears multicoloured, with chunks of text crossed out, and is generally incomprehensible.[142] (-20)	
After several more weeks under the stairs, the PFPM will emerge with something that looks pretty much like the first draft in terms of content but is now four times longer (V0.12).[143] (-20)	Everyone is aligned and everyone has agreed this is what the new project is about, what the anticipated outcomes are and why it's of value to do. (+20)
Further discussion is held before it's accepted that 'it will do for now' once Jim's comments are incorporated.[144] Maya reminds everyone that it's a *living* document and likely to change again so don't finalize it just yet.[145] (-20)	

---

[142] But thanks for all your comments, team.

[143] Save yourself time by not asking about versions 0.2-0.11.

[144] It's always Jim. And always followed by a wee wink and a laugh that suggest to you he thinks he's not asking for much.

[145] Ten-minute discussion follows on whether we now have a V1.0 that may change or if we're still on V0 point something as it's not yet final final.

Estimated time to complete the brief: 8–12 weeks	*Estimated time to complete 5Ps™: 10–20 minutes*
Estimated total resource effort 5–10 days	*Estimated total resource effort 2–4 hours*
Number of track changes – umpteen[146]	*Number of track changes? None*
Next you save the draft/final brief in the system and eventually, after about 12 weeks and 46 versions everyone's energy will peter out and it will finally be agreed as final final (but still a living document, Maya points out).[147] (-20)	Next you decide as a team whether you need to write the brief up.
	Does it need writing up because that's how we do things or because it's actually, actually, actually required for other reasons and needs signing off by some big-wig? Who's going to read it? Who's going to shout if it isn't a formalized document?
On the plus side, governance needs are met as it's in the system so the project now has a RAG status that will need reporting on quarterly (because things that need reporting only happen at quarter end).[148] (-20)	If you've captured the 5Ps™ virtually, then the team can come back to review/amend as needed. (+20)
It's likely to have an irrelevant KPI asking whether it's on track or not, and if this becomes red you'll be shouted at rather than given any help to get it back on track. (-20)	Only write it up if it's really necessary.
	But… if it does need to be written up…

---

[146] Interesting fact totally unrelated: Have you ever wondered why many things in the Bible last a period of 40? Jesus in the wilderness for 40 days. Moses in the desert for 40 years. Noah on his ark for 40 days. You probably haven't but Sami did, so looked it up and it turns out the actual word used is the equivalent of umpteen. Umpteen just means a large number but when translated specifically means 40. Ali-Baba and the 40 thieves. There are umpteen examples.

[147] Even Jim.

[148] No, no they don't.

	Estimated time to write up, review and sign off of around two hours, given you've all already agreed and approved the content as a team. Feedback on the formal document will be small improvements rather than umpteen tracked changes. (+20)
Round 2 score – how did you do?	
Total points available: (-200)	Total points available: (+160)
Round 3 – I just Gantt get enough	
You need a project timeline. Or a Gantt chart if you're being fancy. Without a project plan how will you all know who's doing what and when? Without a proper project plan how will you know what the critical path is? (-20) After some discussion you send the PFPM back to a dark cupboard under the stairs to create a Gantt chart of all the activities that will need to happen over the project lifecycle, including identifying the critical(?) path without which you won't know whether you're in trouble or not. (-20) Eventually the PFPM will emerge, showing they've completed the task by printing it out on several pages of A3 sellotaped together just to	First step, think about the type of change you're doing (page 36). If it's not a Paint by Numbers project don't even think about a detailed project plan because it's highly likely you don't know exactly how you'll do what needs doing even if you do know what the end outcome needs to be. (+20) You can tackle this in a few ways depending on the change type and clarity on the problem that needs fixing: 1: Do a GapLeap™ – capture the gap between where you are and where you'd like to be.[149] Then what will happen if you 'don't

---

[149] Page 84 for a template.

prove how hard it was and how much work it was and how much there is to do to get this project delivered. The critical path is in red. (-20)

It makes little sense to anyone.

Jim helpfully points out that that's because you rescheduled this meeting by two weeks so the chart is already out of date but that it won't take much to update it and hopefully it won't affect the critical path. (-20)

fix it' (impact), what will happen if you 'fix it' (benefits/outcomes) and why it 'hasn't been fixed yet'. Prioritize the reasons why it's 'not fixed yet' in an order that makes sense. You can even cost out each sticky to get the value at stake of not doing the project (fixing the gap) and the cost of fixing some of the 'why not fixed' priorities.[150] (+20)

Only then should you start looking at ideas. Ideas that will fix the 'why not fixed'. This means the ideas will relate to the problem statement (gap) rather than a perceived problem that hasn't really been thought through.[151]

If you have lots of ideas prioritize using ChunkIt!™[152] Plot them relative to each other based on the benefit they'll deliver (high/low) vs the effort they'll take to deliver (high/

---

[150] How much will it cost if you do nothing plus cost benefits if fixed minus cost of fixing?

[151] A good example here is something like culture change… we need to change our culture to be more agile… but why? What's the actual big problem that needs fixing? What isn't getting delivered or done? The problem, if defined well, will likely have other solutions that may be easier to do than changing culture.

[152] Page 210 for a template.

	low) and agree which chunks you should start with.[153] (+20)
	Next take the activity you think you want to start with and use a StickySteps™.[154] (+20)
	First imagine you've already delivered it. What's the end point?
	In order to have delivered x...
	Before then agreeing what you need to do to have achieved this end point; for example, researched, investigated, compiled.
	Put them in order. *Et voila*, you have a high-level project plan for the first activity chunk.
	If the first thing on the plan feels like a big activity, do another StickySteps™, moving this to the top:
	In order to have investigated...
	We must have...
	And repeat the process.

---

[153] It's recommended you don't start with those things that are high effort and low benefit. But you're smart. You've already that figured out.

[154] Page 212 for a template.

You'll end up with a plan of manageable tasks you can work on to get you started towards the first chunk without doing things that may or may not be needed in the longer term. (+20)

Agree who's going to do what before you meet up again. Because the tasks are manageable they're likely to get done. Before you meet up again. No one is worrying about a big activity they've been assigned with a six-month deadline and no idea how to do it. (+20)

When you next meet you'll have progressed the actual project (and not just the paperwork). You don't need to write a report about it. It's happened. So you can go back to your StickySteps™ and see what you need to focus on next. (+20)

This way, if things change through the course of the project, especially if your change is a Quest or Fog, you won't have done any work on future things that may or may not be needed. You'll have just moved it on week by week, making decisions based on what you've done, what you've learned, what you've discovered, before agreeing the next step.

Sami's Fables Part 9

	Be warned though. Jim is still likely to ask about the critical path quite a bit.
Round 3 score – how did you do?	
Total points available: (-80)	Total points available: (+140)
Round 4 – What a difference a day makes	
You typically have monthly, bi-monthly or quarterly project meetings because things happen in monthly or bi-monthly or quarterly cycles. [155] (-20)

That's unless Jim is on leave, or Maya has called in sick requiring you to rearrange and issue a Doodle poll. Again.[156] (-20)

This means decisions can be delayed and issues not dealt with as they arise. It also means progress can be slow as it depends on everyone being there before you can have a meeting, where you're likely to carry forward all the actions as no one has done much since the last meeting due to all the necessary paperwork required for the meeting. (-20) | Agree a day and time, say, Tuesdays at 3pm that everyone can mostly make.[157]

Keep it short – 30 mins could be enough, and use a digital space to capture outputs as you go.[158] (+20)

Do a Hopes&Fears™.

Get rid of the fears – agree actions if needed.

Work through the hopes – doing whatever is needed to achieve them in the meeting.

Agree the 'what next' (manageable) actions and agree who will do them and *et voila* (again).

If Maya can't make it, she can see what you did when she's |

---

[155] Still no one knows if this is two per month or one every two months.

[156] Be warned. This will play havoc with your critical path.

[157] The Prof calls it a 'drumbeat'. It very quickly becomes a habit, so no one forgets because they don't need to look in their calendar to remember it's on.

[158] Unless you have access to a dedicated physical space just for this project.

	back on her feet as it's all held digitally where everyone can access it. (+20)
	If Jim knows he's going to be absent he can drop in a note or summary of what he's delivered on the digital whiteboard, or in the shared update folder before he jets off to Torremolinos. (+20)
	You'll quickly get into the habit of meeting at this time and won't need reminders or rescheduling.
	You'll quickly get in the habit of only adding agenda items (hopes) that are current and need focus.
	You'll quickly get in the habit of short meetings that do the doing and agreeing the next activities rather than having a retrospective every meeting about what *has* happened. (+20)
	You quickly learn how to work asynchronously and know that Jim or Maya being absent won't impact on the critical path that Jim still thinks is needed. (+20)
	You'll be putting all your effort and energy into the project tasks rather than all the associated project management admin and reviewing that projects seem to require an awful lot of. (+20)

Round 4 score – how did you do?	
Total points available: (-60)	Total points available: (+120)
Round 5 – If only we had more admin support	
Admin support is always a challenge, isn't it? There's never enough. But some poor soul (ideally not the PFPM, as they need a break) is asked to capture everything that happened in the project meeting and send it out before the next meeting. (-20)	You meet regularly now, at least weekly but only for a brief time. (+20)
The next meeting will then waste a good 15 minutes of going through this summary to check and agree that it's a good reflection of what happened at the last meeting (with that meeting checking on the summary of the meeting before that…). (-20)	The Hopes&Fears™ keep you focused on what needs doing and killing aliens. (+20)
	At the end of the meeting you've agreed your actions and captured them where everyone can see. (+20)
	You then invite everyone to volunteer for the actions and put their name up. (+20)
Both Jim and Maya will require some amendments on the summary that will get amended and reissued for clarity before filing it as final. (-20)	There's an even split of work based on what everyone can commit to and what everyone likes doing. (+20)
	There's trust that actions will get done and there's support if people are struggling because you're all aligned and have shared goals. (+20)
Then 30 minutes will be spent reviewing the actions and agreeing to carry most of them forward to the next meeting because everyone's been so busy writing things up, they haven't had time to do any real work. (-20)	The actions are manageable and make sense in relation to progressing the project even if the end goal is still a little unclear. (+20)

Everyone will then get up in a rush to get to their next meeting because risk is next on the agenda. (-20)	You'll find that actions get done without you having to chase or check they've been done. (+20) *Et,* dare I say it again, *voila*.
Round 5 score – how did you do?	
Total points available: (-100)	Total points available: (+160)

Time to add up your scores. How did you do? (The score range is -540 to +700).
Total Score _____

Ninja moves

> Don't worry if you have a very less than 0 score. This is perfectly normal. This is what Sami sees everywhere and why Sami thought it might be useful to share different approaches. Sami wasn't optimistic it would do anything at an organization level because there are just too many experts with certificates in processes that should be followed to the letter for delivering change activities.[159] Sami

---

[159] Sami had a few of these certificates also. It wasn't that the training was bad but mostly the approaches seemed to be common sense wrapped up in lots of jargon, and when being applied in the work setting Sami often observed there was more effort on jargon and dogmatic use of process than using a common-sense approach with some appropriate levels of structure and governance. The risk management process was a shining example of this.

> anticipates it will largely be ignored in favour of the next buzzword bandwagon.
>
> But you, you have no excuses now. You know many of the Ninja moves that are needed to make real change happen. And while it may take time to convince others (don't beat yourself up too much if it's slow going), you can start small fires burning, get fellow pirates on board, and start with some stealth-like actions.

Tools and templates

Bin the agenda

Don't decide on behalf of the team what you think they need to do three weeks in advance of a meeting. Ask them at the start of the meeting. Most importantly, ask them about their fears and get rid of them before you start the meeting proper.

- Everyone will feel more relaxed if the fears have been dealt with.
- Everyone will feel more aligned if the 'agenda' is their agenda and focused on what needs to be done today.
- It saves time and admin.

- It ensures everyone is focused during the meeting on what actually needs doing. Today, now.
- You're much more likely to focus on doing the doing rather than talking about what you might do or talking about what you've done since you last met.[160]

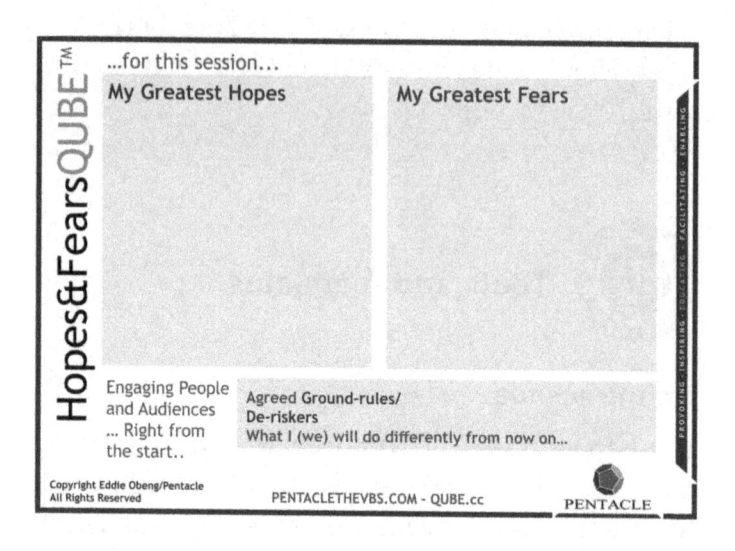

---

[160] While it's important to look back, reflect, share success, the balance is often the wrong way round, with meetings focusing on the past rather than looking forward. Imagine driving a car like this, mostly looking in the rear-view mirror rather than at the road ahead. What could possibly go wrong?

Team catch-up

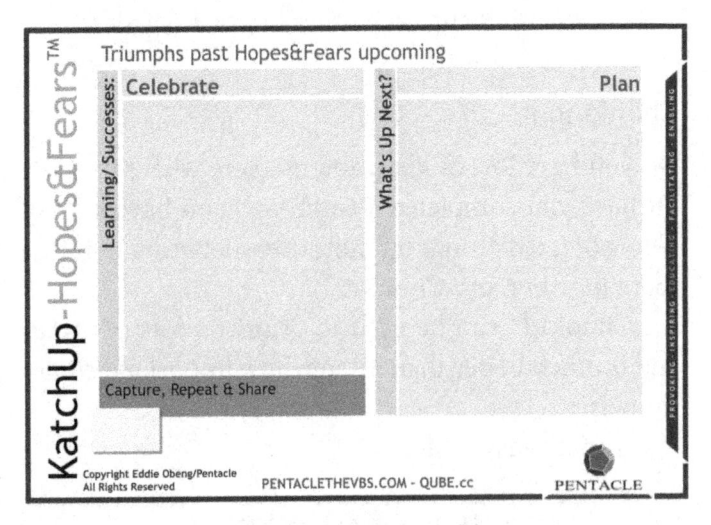

![KatchUp-Hopes&Fears template with quadrants: Celebrate, Plan, Learning/Successes, What's Up Next?, and Capture, Repeat & Share]

Ideal for regular quick team catch-ups. Instead of getting people to do presentations and write reports, use KatchUp™. Instead of needing a good couple of hours to give everyone their 15-minute slot, meet more often but for, say, 15 minutes twice a week. Get everyone to write first then just highlight what they need to highlight.

- You all get to celebrate the good stuff that's happened very recently; that is, in the last couple of days.
- You all know who needs help and on what over the next couple of days.
- You meet more frequently so things are less likely to go wrong or be missed.
- You spend less time overall in meetings.

- You'll start to email each other less as you know you're seeing each other in just a day or two.

Chunking it

Do you have lots of ideas and not sure where to start? Or have you completed a GapLeap™ and have a lot of 'why not fixed' things but not sure what order to tackle them in? Then use ChunkIt!™

ChunkIt!™ can be used to prioritize lots of things and is much better than asking 'how important' something is.

And it's easy to do.

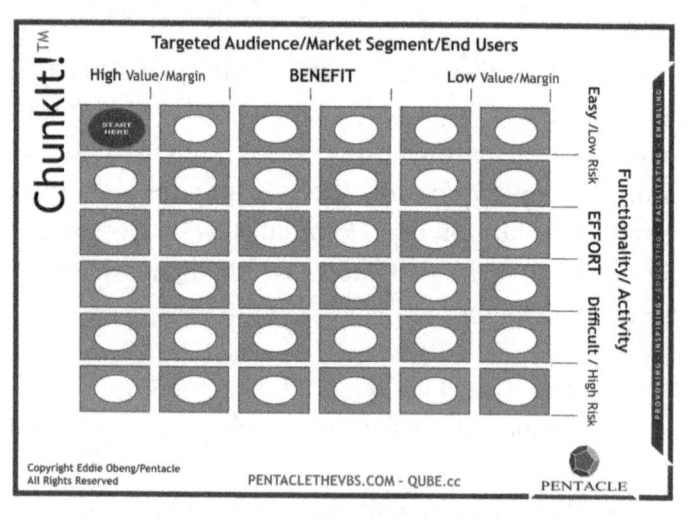

Take your list of things you need to prioritize and plot them based on how much effort is needed to do them vs how much benefit they'll deliver. Place them relative to each other and agree where to start – ideally the low effort/high benefit. You may start with a high effort/high benefit and forego all the other things. The point is that it allows sensible discussion on what you will (or can) do and what you'll put aside for now.

Spend the rest of the meeting wondering why you didn't think of doing it this way in the first place.

Backwards planning

Remember that Gantt chart... the one that's out of date before it's even printed off? The one that likely started from 'here' and plotted a path to 'there' with 'there' being much further into the future than you can possibly imagine.

And remember the types of change descriptions?[161]

Well unless what you're doing is a Paint by Numbers type of change where you know what you need to deliver and know how you'll do it, then a long-term detailed plan is pretty useless.

Instead use StickySteps™. This helps you plan the next steps and specific actions without thinking too far ahead. It's essential in any project that isn't totally clear on the *how* or *what*.

First transport yourself to the future of the thing you're certain you need to do. For a project that's Foggy or a Quest your first step needs to be something tangible. Imagine your end goal is to become an innovative organization but you don't yet know what this means or how to do it. You can't possibly do

---

[161] Paint by Numbers, Movie, Quest, Fog.

a long-term plan. But you can start with a short first step that might be 'to understand what we mean by innovation in our organization'.

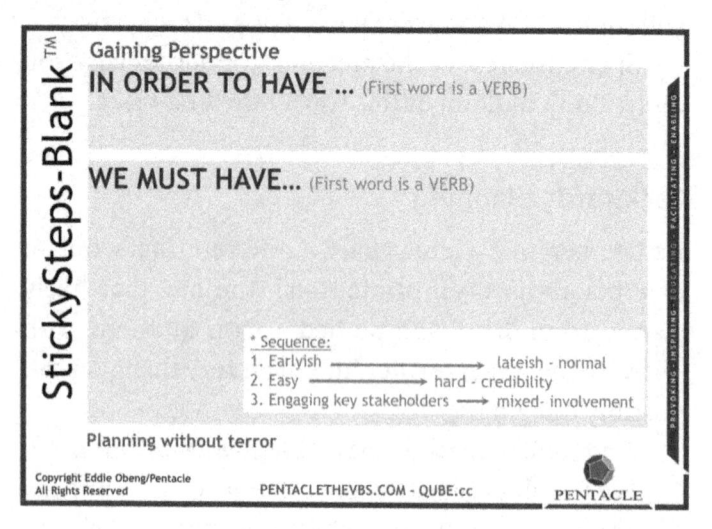

> **StickySteps-Blank™**
>
> Gaining Perspective
> **IN ORDER TO HAVE ...** (First word is a VERB)
>
> **WE MUST HAVE...** (First word is a VERB)
>
> *Sequence:
> 1. Earlyish ———→ lateish - normal
> 2. Easy ———→ hard - credibility
> 3. Engaging key stakeholders ——→ mixed- involvement
>
> Planning without terror
>
> Copyright Eddie Obeng/Pentacle
> All Rights Reserved PENTACLETHEVBS.COM - QUBE.cc PENTACLE

So… to have understood what we mean by innovation, we must have…

- Researched innovation in similar organizations
- Interviewed managers
- Understood what areas need innovation
- Interviewed stakeholders

These are all shortish-term actions that can be put in an order that makes sense as a plan, agreed and assigned. They might still feel quite big actions so you can repeat the process with each 'big action'.

In order to have interviewed managers, we must have…

- Identified which managers to interview
- Sent out calendar invites for interviews
- Agreed a set of interview questions
- Checked that the interview questions will give us answers we need

And so on.[162]

Using verbs turns the ideas into actions, so you have an immediate to-do list that you've all worked on together and agreed that these are the first priorities. And no one is worried about the 'what by when' for year three.[163]

You should ideally be aiming for a plan that covers actions that could be done in the next one to three weeks.

Your reflection

Wow. That was an eye-opener. You circled your scores as you went but you did it twice. You used a red pen to score for the meetings or projects you had no influence over but had to attend and 'play the game'. You used

---

[162] This is also really helpful on Fog or Quest types of change for people who prefer the PbN type of change. Overall the change is still unclear but you've made the first bit a mini PbN activity, which means you can progress the first step *and* make those in the team who like PbN activities less anxious.

[163] Well, no one in the team. The Mini-Cheddars at that first workshop may still likely demand a three-year action plan.

a green pen for the ones you lead or could influence or where you were helping others to lead in different ways. Your red score was pretty negative. Soooo negative that you don't want to share it. You knew the old ways were bad but hadn't quite anticipated how bad. No wonder your energy was sapped in these meetings.

But the green score is pretty healthy. You don't always get it right, and some of the teams you work with don't want to ditch all their old practices in one go, but each week you're making iterative steps forward with these teams to get them working in these new ways. You're confidently scoring over 300 in all the areas you can influence and over 500 in the areas you're leading. You feel a sense of both relief and exhilaration that you've managed to get this far given the little support you've had from the senior decision-makers. Time to continue the journey.

Challenge 9

Continued...

So... back to the three curious requests this week.

The first is from a dispersed group of people who want to learn this stuff so you arrange three training sessions to teach them how to run their own drumbeats, shift how they run meetings, and apply these new tools to create the new work behaviours and team culture.[164]

It's like learning a new language (which can seem odd at first) but when you go to live in the country where they speak that language it quickly all starts to make sense. You give them the tools *and* the language. You also have a lot of fun.[165] They then go off to share it more widely with the teams they work with. This is another example of the organic spread of new ways of working you'd imagined.

The second request requires help writing a business case for a large (£40ish million) replacement laboratory IT system. They can't face the months of meetings and pulling together of requirements documentation and all the opinions and squabbling that it will entail. Plus the team is already busy and don't have the time.

---

[164] Based on Sami's Quiz.
[165] Too often absent in training.

You offer to facilitate their project meetings if they're happy to work virtually and apply the new tools and approaches you've been learning how to use to speed up delivery.

Six weeks later they have, using the tools mentioned within this book, developed a high-level proposal solution based on user needs (human-centred design process), got the grumpy IT and finance stakeholders on board (IDQB™), rattled through a business case (GapLeap™), benefits, risks *and* produced a document (for governance purposes) but with *no* tracked changes). All in just six weeks with just one hour per week of getting together. It sails through the board meeting, gets signed off and eventually becomes not just a business case for a regional replacement IT system but a national business case.

And the final request is from a group of smart people. The kind of people who have to be smart. To do their jobs well. Because their job directly impacts on their customers.[166] And because they're smart, they know lots of things. So, their opinions are well informed and backed up by data. Which is great. That's until you end up with five of them in the same room trying to resolve an issue that they sort of agree exists but they all have a slightly different opinion on what the right answer is.

So, when you're invited in to help, you know a new approach is needed. The sponsor asks you for ideas, particularly as she knows another half-day workshop

---

[166] In this case patients. Or more specifically surgical patients.

will only achieve more frustration and lack of progress. You agree to get them hooked up to work together virtually and again use the tools you've learned to align them on what the actual problem is, which turns out to be a bit different to what they thought the problem was.[167] They then agree what's needed to fix the problem, develop a prototype solution they test locally with their teams (having killed the aliens first), before making some adjustments to agree a final product.[168] Just three weeks later (again after meeting for just an hour a week) they go away happy, particularly as individually they feel like they've got the solution they thought was the right answer in the first place.

Et... voila...

Current status ☻ 99 ☺ 3

It's a couple of weeks later and, despite all the good things that have happened, you still feel as if you're taking one step forward and two back. You're still at odds with most of the Mini Cheddars, and the Boss is now on your back.

Last week you led a collaboration of health innovations for a big national public event of around 2,000 attendees. Instead of the usual 'organizational conference-type stand' you gathered lots of different people involved in innovation and then you all developed an interactive, fun, insightful exhibition showcasing lots

---

[167] Remember, this is still a novel way to work, and when it's used it's mostly for meetings, not for actually working on projects to deliver outcomes.

[168] Hopes&Fears™, GapLeap™, 5Ps™, Fix-It-NOW™ are all used.

of health innovations. You all agreed that as this was a true collaboration it needed its own branding, rather than it all sitting under the umbrella of one leading (i.e. your) organization. Especially as its intent was to inform and capture insights from the public, who wouldn't, primarily, know who that organization was. It was hugely popular, lots of data was captured to help with future ideas, the Minister for Innovation invited you to write up the story to include in their blog and a video you made goes viral(ish). It was the true definition of successful collaboration.

Until Monday morning....

Your inbox is full of 'thank yous' and 'well dones'. But the Boss is grimacing and requests your presence in their office. They're not happy. And why? Because it wasn't clear that your organization was 'leading the event'. Despite it being a collaboration 'it should have been clear', they say, 'especially to the minister at least' (even though by default they know your organization 'led it' because you've written the blog for them).

'But... collaboration...' you start to mutter before realizing there's no point.

As you leave you remember Sami's Fable about killer wasps and the collaboration event and how nobody got it. Collaboration is still, it seems, a dark art for many.

It's not what you'd expected and the wind is knocked out of you.

Current status 🕐 41 ◐2

You decide to go for a walk to have a think. You get surprised looks when you put on your coat as it's only

Challenge 9 Continued...

mid-morning and it's not the norm to go for a walk during office hours.

You start to think about everything. At first you start to doubt yourself. You're often criticized for doing what you think is the right thing to do, which makes you wonder *is it me or them*? more often than you think is healthy. You accept you break the rules, are slightly unorthodox in approaches but isn't that the point of your role? To challenge the usual and try new things?

You also think back to the zoo event and how hard that was, how much you felt compromised because you had to go along with the suggested way rather than the way you thought was right.

You start to wonder again whether it's time for a new adventure. Have you reached the end of what you can do here? That amazing challenging programme start you started with has pretty much disappeared. The only recognizable bit that really happened was changing people's job titles and the org charts, the legacy of which, at least for many staff, is still palatably painful.[169] Here you are, doing things to support those aims on the posters for innovation, agility, empowerment, and the powers that be seem to be trying to stop you at every turn.

You head back to your desk, and rather than sit at your laptop pick up Sami's Fables and head back outside. It's a nice day and you can go and sit on a bench somewhere to pick up where you left off. More surprised stares follow you as you walk out of Grey Quarters.

---

[169] Oh, and that one shiny gadget project, which, you accept, was good, but it's still only one project.

Sami's Fables Part 10

If it makes sense, it's probably sense-making

Sami was having a tough week. Nothing Sami did, it seemed, was the right thing. But rather than getting frustrated, Sami decided instead to reflect on their very first project.

This project was long before formal project management processes had been introduced in the organization. Where PRINCE2 was the name for the artist formerly known as PRINCE.

Sami had been assigned a task to lead a project to develop a data warehouse, which was also quite a new thing in the world of IT.

Sami had zero idea where to start so asked someone in IT to help.

'Oh, well, you need a database first,' they said. 'You can't have a data warehouse without a database.' Sami was still clueless but now clueless about where to start on two things.

'So,' asked Sami, 'where should I start?'

'You need a user requirement document,' they said. 'I'll send you a sample one you can use as a template.'

A 300-page document subsequently landed in Sami's inbox.

Sami groaned. Quite, quite loudly.

Sami now had three things to do that Sami didn't really understand. Sami decided this needed drastic action and creative thinking.

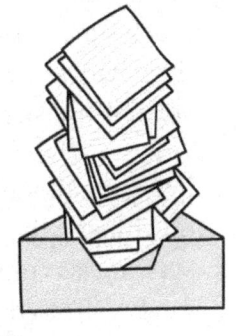

Who would be the best person to write down what's needed for this database? Sami thought. Those that would be putting data in the database, the main users of the system, seemed to be the most obvious and logical answer.

So Sami invited all the users to a free lunch, persuaded an IT database guru to come along and explained the challenge.[170]

---

[170] Sadly, not a hot buffet. Budgets didn't stretch that far. More the kind of beige buffet that's also commonly seen at events. You know, the ones full of beige food, disguised as healthy with the odd sprig of parsley and a soggy tomato.

Sami then asked the database guru to mock up a database on the presentation screen and asked the users to tell them what they wanted in it.[171]

After the session, the database guru took the mock-up and used it as a basis to do the first step in the database design. A few repeat sessions later... *et voila*. A user-designed system.

Everyone thought Sami was nuts. 'That's not how we do things!' the Blockers screamed quietly. But the system was coming along nicely, and the users were mighty pleased to be involved and excited that they were getting a brand-new database and reporting system that reflected their needs. It was at this point that Sami was starting to be talked about as a troublemaker.

But Sami was feeling quite smug and thinking that their database project was about complete and could be deemed a success. Until, that is, the IT manager alerted them to yet another task.

'We need a UAT document,' said the IT manager.

---

[171] Okay, so you're thinking this is just user design. Nothing new to see here. But back then, in the times of yore, user design wasn't a thing. Filling in documents was the thing. By yourself in a dark room. Remember, at this point in time, PRINCE2 wasn't a common thing, and agile was something ballet dancers were good at.

'A what?' asked Sami.

'A user acceptance testing document. You need to tell us how we'll check it does what it's meant to. For every data entry field, you need to describe what it should do and what it shouldn't. And then you need to test all the data fields and check them against this list to check they do what they should do and don't do what they shouldn't. I'll send you a sample one you can use as a template.'

Sami groaned. People were now used to Sami's groaning, so nobody paid any attention. Subsequently a 300-page document appeared in Sami's inbox. Sami groaned again, and again it fell on deaf ears.

But Sami's confidence had grown. *There must be an easier way*, thought Sami.

So Sami invited the users back for another free lunch. Then set up a bunch of laptops with the beta product and got them to, well, user-test it and write down what didn't work or needed changing. They were, after all, the experts in what they needed the thing to do and not do.

'That's not how we do things!' screamed the Blockers quietly, but again this method worked and again the users were excited about the new system and how much better it was than the old one and how they couldn't wait to start using it once it was rolled out.[172]

Sami started to celebrate again. But still it was too soon.

'There's still one big last task,' said the IT manager. 'We need to shut down the old database, which is no longer required. You'll need to find out who *all* the users are and contact them to let them know before we switch over. Unfortunately, we don't know who they all are so it could take some time to find them. We think there are a lot of people out there who access it for reports.

'Once you do find them, we'll need them to fill in the appropriate documentation to access the new system before we can transfer them over. Only then can we switch off the old system and stop using it. Until then we have to maintain both systems, which means double entry of the data because the systems don't talk to each other.

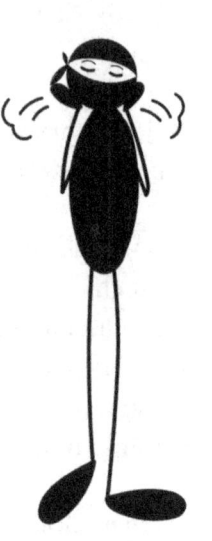

---

[172] Sami didn't realize at the time that this reaction was rare and most people didn't get excited by new systems because they knew, from experience, that new systems rarely did what was needed from the user perspective.

This caused Sami some head-scratching. How could they not know who uses it when they issue passwords and have such rigid access protocols? And why did they not mention this sooner? But Sami has worked with IT long enough now to know that logical questions rarely got the answer needed but did get further riddles to solve.

Sami felt frustrated, particularly for the main users, who had put so much effort into the new system and would now be asked to do double the work until the old one could be switched off.

But Sami was also feeling brave and creative problem-solving had worked pretty well on this project so far.

First, Sami asked those who designed and tested the new system who else might use the system. They provided a very short list of names and Sami quickly contacted them and got them onboarded to the new system.

Then, Sami made an executive decision.

'Just switch it off,' Sami said. 'If someone currently uses it and finds it not working, they'll soon let us know and we can give them access to the new one.'

'That's not how we do things!' screamed the Blockers, quite loudly this time, and the two of them went into battle with Sami but Sami won and so it was done.

Oddly, there wasn't a peep from anyone about the old database being unavailable.

Ninja moves

> ### Keep challenging the status quo
>
> Today, much of this approach seems obvious and common practice. We call it agile, co-design, user design and all manner of things.
>
> Time has moved on and we're much better in general at this approach, but at the time, it just made sense to Sami to do it this way. It saved a whole lot of time and energy in trying to do it the traditional way (and likely getting it wrong) and everyone was happy (apart from the IT Manager and the Blockers).
>
> If you have an idea how to do something, if it feels like the right way, then try it. First identify the

aliens so you can de-risk it as much as possible.[173] If something feels like it's the wrong way, then challenge it, but again identify aliens first. Learn as you go, de-risking what you can.[174] Think about what will happen next if you do a certain thing using ISWON™.[175] Don't follow dogma but do follow your instincts if the 'what will happen next' seems like it will be a good thing.

You don't need a certificate in something to be able to do something (although some courses are useful to do).

Equally, a certificate in something doesn't mean you can do it well. It just means you can rote learn,

---

[173] I remember several years ago there was a chap who decided to parachute to earth from space. I also remember everyone talking about how risky this was and that there was a big chance he would die. But on reading about the project, I realized that much of the work they did in the years leading up to this point was to de-risk the project to the point that it wasn't that risky at all. They thought about *everything* that might go wrong and de-risked it. Things are often only risky if you haven't done anything to de-risk them. Kill the aliens up front and there's a good chance you'll be just fine. Focus on risk management process without doing much about the risks proper and there's a good chance you won't be just fine. If you know people who just seem to breeze through life, there's a very good chance they're very good at de-risking things; you just don't see this bit.

[174] It's quite possible this 'right' way will become a recognized accredited process at some point in the future. Be warned, though, as it too will be applied with dogma and all common sense will fly out the window.

[175] Page 63.

> pass an exam and possibly talk about it in a knowledgeful way while hiding behind jargon.
>
> But remember, when it works (and it will, not always but you'll learn things when it doesn't) don't gloat or be a smartarse. Invisible leadership is one of the key moves a Change Ninja can make.
>
> Just keep a note of it and maybe write about it many years later.

Tools and templates

How was it for you?

Sami has one last tool for you. And it can be used for everything you do. Everything. You know those lessons learned sessions often set up at the very end of very long projects? The projects that overran, possibly are still pilots but no longer a 'project'. The original team long since disappeared. The sessions where you sit in a room capturing all the things you should have done differently. And would do differently if you had to do it again. And some poor soul translates all those sticky notes into a giant spreadsheet that's saved in spreadsheet heaven (in the folder where ideas go to die). Well, you can keep doing that and never really learn or…

ActionReplay™

Build a secure Future by Reflecting on the Past

	Worked well?	Failed?
Planned?	Why did it work? How can we do more?	Why did it fail? What can we do differently next time?
Not Planned?	Why did this happen? How can we repeat it?	Why did this go wrong? How can we avoid it in future?

Actions: Capture the answers/actions here

Reflections:

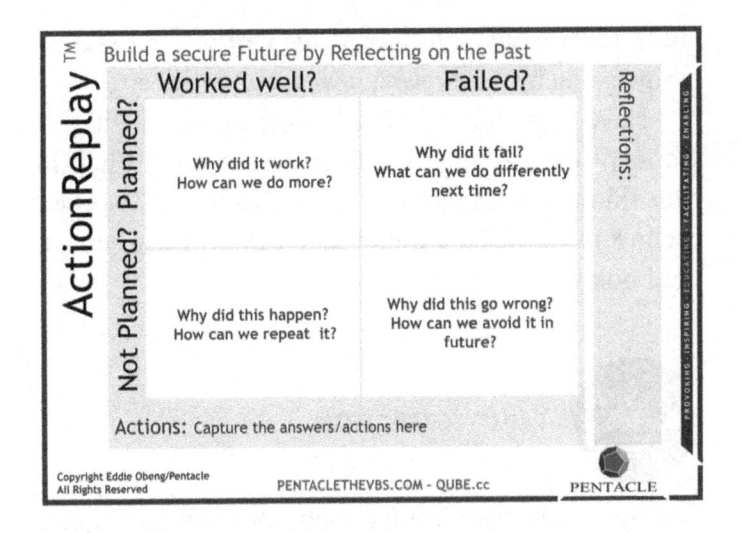

Copyright Eddie Obeng/Pentacle — All Rights Reserved — PENTACLETHEVBS.COM - QUBE.cc — PENTACLE

... you could do an action replay, say, every four to six weeks for a project or after any event or big meeting.

- Start top-left and go round clockwise capturing what happened.
- Agree actions to do the good stuff again/more of.
- Agree actions to avoid the bad stuff happening again.
- Build these actions into your StickySteps™ project plan.
- Finish on the worked well and not planned. These things *always* feel good.

This way you learn as you go, correcting mistakes to avoid them happening again and build on all the good things that happen. It happens in real time so you can apply the learning immediately, you get to build team skills and knowledge and get the endorphins going by celebrating how great you all are.

Have a go now... What's worked well with this book? What did you plan to do that failed? What do you think was unplanned but, in your eyes, worked well? You can let me know, as I'll use it for feedback for book two!

Your reflection

You appreciate Sami's story about the database is quite old and things have moved on, with that approach being fairly common now. But it really resonates with your journey. You're constantly being told by the Blockers, the Mini Cheddars, the Digital Transformation Director, the Steely Governance Manager and even the Boss that this is not how we do things but you've persevered because it felt right. If it went wrong you learned, if it went well, you did more of it.

There might not be a specific course to attend and certificate you can collect (yet) on this approach but it felt and still feels like the right approach. Especially as it's all about collaboration and people. And if you use ActionReplay™ as you go then everyone will learn together, which will increase confidence in doing the 'right thing' even if it's not the done thing. This has given you the energy and oomph you need to go into your final challenge.

Challenge 10

Hack to the future[176]

It's a couple of weeks later and it's a full weekend of work. Why are you working at the weekend? Well, it's what has become the regular hackathon.[177] Hackathon 3. This one is in a sports centre with the huge hall being used for various different activities.

---

[176] Shamelessly stolen the name from a team at the NHS Project Futures five-day hack... you know who you are.

[177] A hackathon is a great way to get free resources. That's not the formal definition but it's mine. Essentially you book out a long weekend somewhere, invite lots of people to attend to work on some challenge questions (often this is for digital solutions but doesn't need to be), then invite some organizations to set some real challenge questions and let the participants form teams, produce ideas and develop solutions. The participants need feeding regularly, but ideally not after midnight. You'll also need to provide some support and mentoring so they can learn new skills, such as user design, pitching ideas and creating business cases. After a couple of days you'll find that you have a bunch of prototype solutions for some very real problems. Like I said, free resource. Well nearly. You'll have to chip in for the price of a few pizzas.

The 50-plus teams have been set up at one end of the hall, squashed up tight, and multiple organizations and mentors are set up at stations around the hall walls. One corner has been set up with a mini stage for various talks throughout the weekend. People are everywhere, progressing their ideas, talking to experts, carrying out user insight interviews or trying to shoot basketballs into a net. You've just finished a LEGO® Serious Play® workshop in one of the break-out spaces (with the requisite bean bags) where many ideas were generated for teams to then progress. You grab some tea, find a quiet(ish) spot in the corner of the sports hall and sit down on a wooden balance bench.

This year's 'Data Hack' has broken all expectations regarding numbers, sponsors, organizations involved and number of staff attending. You even have a minister attending on Sunday to announce the awards. You start to reflect on previous hacks and your innovation journey, successes and failures.

You recall when you first mooted the idea of a data hackathon for the organization. There was very little enthusiasm. The Digital Transformation Director even queried why you'd be encouraging the hacking of data.[178] But as with other innovation ideas you'd worked on you talked to a lot of people, got some

---

[178] You accept not everyone is familiar with the term data hacks but you did expect the leader of all things digital and transformative to know that this was a method that had been around for a while to develop new ideas using technology.

managers interested and created enough of a backing to forge ahead.

For the first event you'd anticipated 40 or so attendees. Over 80 registered. Some even flew in for the weekend. And some brought tents and slept in the venue all weekend. The Mini Cheddars showed little interest but didn't stop it. The Blockers told you it was a waste of time. Jim, to be fair, did make an appearance on the last night for the presentations.[179] And then, on day two, social media started doing what it does best and created a real buzz. Without any planning, some very Big Cheeses from other organizations started popping in over the weekend doing impromptu talks, which were quickly loaded on to social media to get even more interest. This was huge. The atmosphere, the buzz, the number of ideas and coding that was achieved in just three days was incredible.

But back in the office on Monday there was still very little interest in what might have happened, although the Boss did seem to be aware of who had randomly 'popped in'. And this did prompt them to later share the event video in the right places to the right people to show that they *were* supportive of the idea.

Hack 2 was a repeat. But on a bigger scale. And with more emphasis on internal staff taking part. To work on real organizational problems. There was bigger interest from the Boss, and a couple of the Mini Cheddars too, who all wanted to be on the

---

[179] Although you're not sure if this was because he was interested or because he heard there was going to be free pizza and beer.

judging panel or have a role where they would be 'seen'. Maya even offered to take part in mentoring the teams. Jackpot.

Hack 3 and here you are. You're no longer needed and you're really here just to observe and provide some mentorship to teams. You've handed the baton on to others. You're still amazed at how many people are willing to give up their entire weekend to work solidly on the challenges.

So, the hacks have been a success. As was QUBE, the Prof's tools, virtual working, LSP, human-centred design and creative problem-solving methodologies. They were all people-orientated rather than shiny gadget-orientated. You took a bottom-up approach, giving staff the tools and confidence to do their job better, to explore and introduce new methods and ideas, to shift behaviours and how teams did things. It wasn't about telling staff they were empowered but about giving them the tools, confidence, space and environment so they could actually feel empowered to do different things and spread the learning wider.

It was a hard slog to get any of it accepted, things didn't always quite do what you'd hoped but they were all worth pushing and sticking with and here you are reflecting on the impact and outcomes. It might not look like innovation or transformation for many but those small fires burning everywhere are definitely leading to real change in *how* teams are working to deliver real outcomes to real problems, often at speed and often in collaboration with others.

It's also now much bigger than you and has a life of its own. You think back to that original workshop with the giant calendar. You still aren't really sure what you'd put on it even knowing what you now know. But you do know you followed the right path.

So, what next? you wonder. The organization has shifted again, the Big Cheese, who started the big programme, has moved on. So have the good Mini Cheddars. The old soggy and slightly stale Mini Cheddars are still there and seem to be growing in number and trying to revert things back to the good old days. You want to do more of what you're doing but have you reached the end of this particular journey? Are you ready to jump ship and go in search of a new adventure?

Decision time

a) Is it Game Over? (page 237)

Is it Game Over?

Congratulations

It's Game Over. Not in the giving up sense. But in the 'woohoo you made it to the end, well done you' sense. All the way without giving up.[180]

You've battled giants and known when to let go. You've focused on people and helping them reach their own insights. You've spent more time on working on problems than jumping straight to solutions. You've used your gut feel to make decisions. When it went wrong you learned from it and got on with the next task.[181] And you found a crew of like-minded rebels who've supported you through this.

---

[180] Well maybe you did give up but you got back on that saddle and here you are.

[181] And learned that this is called 'smart failure'.

You think back to that original workshop. The one with the aims of the transformation programme on tiny bits of paper at the end of the room.

To be more agile – well you've definitely achieved that. Not just for you but for all the teams you've helped along the way, sharing the new tools and ways of working. Not only are they more agile but they keep telling you how much more efficient they are, meaning they can get a lot more value-added activities done with their time.

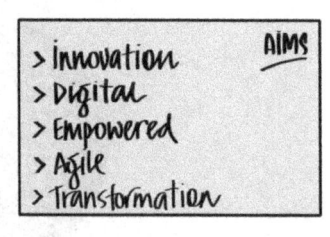

> AIMS
> > innovation
> > Digital
> > Empowered
> > Agile
> > Transformation

To be more innovative – again you've managed to do this. Not in a shiny gadgets way but in an innovate working practice way. You've shifted from 9–5 office working and presenteeism to a blended approach that removes the need for people to be physically together. And this wasn't just about introducing video conferencing technologies.[182] This was about creating a collaborative, safe and fun space, where everyone was autonomous, where tools were easily available to identify real problems, work on ideas, learn and deliver outcomes. The approach you took around shifting behaviours and the tools you applied for changing how

---

[182] Covid happened since these stories. It introduced video conferencing technologies for all. This is not virtual working. It's mostly just the same as before but on a screen. Unless of course you've built-in collaboration tools, new behaviours, shifted from meetings to talk about things to workshopping to do things, and many of the other things mentioned in this book.

teams worked together and how projects were delivered transformed ways of working. As a result, staff feel more confident, teams are open to collaborating across boundaries and willing to try things, knowing that if they fail they'll learn from it. This has resulted in more and more creative ideas and innovative solutions to local challenges being delivered iteratively and at speed.

To empower staff – you've done this too. From the volunteers you recruited to the staff reward and recognition programme. From the small activities like Friday film club to creating peer-supported virtual groups. They're all much braver and more confident in suggesting new things and leading change. And you've felt empowered to learn new tools and facilitate others in using them, from creative problem-solving to user design to LEGO® Serious Play®.

To have a digital workforce – well no one could argue that you've not transformed working practice using an immersive 3D virtual office environment. And for those who argue this is a shiny gadget – it isn't. Yes, there's technology but that's just there to support the humans that use it, the behaviours and culture it creates to do the work that's needed. That is what you think a digital workforce really is about. Human connectedness that uses technology to support humans in doing what they need to do.

There are still plenty of naysayers, the aspiring Mini Cheddars and the Blockers who don't see anything wrong with doing things the way they've always done them. And you can't put an obvious KPI or a RAG status on what you've achieved, so those still in bureaucracy land will never acknowledge the benefits. But you, and all those who are doing things differently, know what the outcomes are and that's all that matters.[183]

With stealth-like Ninja moves you've shifted team cultures, energy, motivation and job satisfaction. And many more are now trained in these tools and approaches. You've created an 'empty room of Change Ninjas'.[184]

It was hard going but you realized:

a) it was the system you were battling against, not people; and
b) dealing with potential people blockers as real people with real thoughts that needed listening to, while time-consuming, was definitely worth the effort for longer-term gain.

You have a great future ahead and are ready for a new adventure. But don't forget what you've learned. Apply the tools immediately.

Sami and Tammy wish you the best of luck with your next adventure.

---

[183] More invisible leadership needed here.
[184] The collective noun for Ninjas. So stealth-like that no one knows they're there.

Appendix of tools

Name of tool	Description	Page
TypesofChange™	What kind of project is it? Do you know *what* you're doing and *how* you need to do it? What type of leadership is needed to manage the team effectively?	36
5Ps™	Aligning the team on the new project/activity/communication	50
ISWON™	Decision-making tool – what will happen next?	63
GapLeap™	Twenty-minute business case	84
SlizedBread™	Making your idea even better	86
IDQB™	Removing emotion to find out what people really object to so you can agree a solution together	106
Human-Centred Design	Finding out what problems your users have before developing ideas, testing prototypes and building solutions	134
Aladin-Journey™	Working through a customer journey to design your product	137
StakeholderGrid2™	What do people/individuals really understand about your project and what might they do as a result?	151
Fix-It-NOW™	How to manage risk and kill 'em dead!	154

Hopes&Fears™	Align the team on what you need to do in the meeting to progress your activities	208
KatchUp™	Use for regular team meetings – celebrate and share what you're doing next	209
ChunkIt!™	Prioritize ideas or actions based on effort and benefit	210
StickySteps™	Planning back from the future – particularly useful for Quests and Foggy projects	212
ActionReplay™	Learn lessons as you go to avoid the things that don't work and do more of the things that do work	229

Recommended reading

There are many books on change management that I could list but you'll know which ones are right for you. For me, the best reading insights I had derived from the 'other' types of books to help me see things from other perspectives and learn how to approach things differently. Here are just a few but these, for me, were both practical and insightful, particularly for understanding the differences between people, which is essential if you want to be a Change Ninja.

All Change – Eddie Obeng. This one has much more detail on the 'process' to follow for the different change types.

Who Killed the Sparq – Eddie Obeng

Be More Pirate – Sami Conniff Allende

How to Be More Pirate – Sami Conniff & The Big Cheese Barker

Busy – Tony Crabbe

Messy – Tim Harford

Drive – Dan Pink

XLR8 – John Kotter

The Checklist Manifesto – Atul Gawande

The Idiot Brain – Dean Burnett

The Coaching Habit – Michael Bungay

Useful resources, methods and toolkits

The LEGO® Serious Play® method is well documented, but Sean Blair's books are particularly practical and a good resource to have when designing sessions.

Systems thinking resources were particularly useful in helping to see, understand and help others with the bigger picture, particularly combined with LEGO® Serious Play®. Both Donella Meadows.org and *Pride and Joy* by Alex Knight provided useful reading and stories for sharing.

Growth mindset, often used in education situations, is particularly useful for your own resilience! But it can also be useful for understanding others and why they might not be quite as enthusiastic as you about the change you're leading. Carol Dweck is a good place to start. An example of this in use is the event at the zoo where participants started with a fixed mindset (arms folded/not playing) and needed to shift to a growth mindset before they would engage properly in the activity.

Human-centred design…

- Free courses at: www.acumenacademy.org/course/design-kit-human-centered-design/)

- Free toolkits at: www.Deisgnkit.org
- Handbook: *Sprint: Solve Big Problems and Test New Ideas in Just Five Days* by Jake Knapp

Nesta is a great source of many toolkits for innovation, collaboration, motivating staff, idea generation. There are too many to suggest which ones here. www.nesta.org.uk/toolkit/

Trying to put habits in place or get a team building new habits? BJ Fogg's *Tiny Habits* is a great place to start.

Cialdini's *Six Principles of Influence or Persuasion* is useful for 'selling' ideas. And as Ninja change manager you need to be very good at 'selling' even if it feels wrong to say it that way. You can read the book or Google for lots of quick videos. Productivity game on YouTube has a great one with associated PDF: www.youtube.com/watch?v=OqyN-HPkyPA

My website with the PET resources can be found here: www.changeninjahandbook.com

Acknowledgements

This journey was hard going at times and sometimes my confidence took a battering, but I had support from some amazing people who coached, mentored, provided opportunity, listened and believed in me, so special thanks to: Eddie Obeng, Moira Mackenzie, Susan Burney, Jo Stanford, Cath Calderwood, Tim Smit, Aileen Keel, Lorna Jackson, Mary Morgan, Emma Hogg, Leo Teixeira, Jacqueline and Harry Cooper, Alex Barker, Susan Ross, Sean Blair.

Thank you to all the Pirates and Volunteers who played a part in making this happen and are very much part of this story. You know who you are.

Enormous thanks to early readers who gave amazing feedback to help whip this book into shape. Andrew Brooks, Jonathan Norman, Shara Seeyave, Fi Strachan, Molly Thomas. And finally thank you Vanessa Randle for your inspiring illustrations and the team at PIP for all your support, help and encouragement. It has made the process of getting this book out there a very enjoyable experience.